THE WAR OF THE TWO BROTHERS

The War of the Two Brothers

The Portuguese Civil War 1828-1834

Sérgio Veludo Coelho

Helion & Company

Helion & Company Limited
Unit 8 Amherst Business Centre
Budbrooke Road
Warwick
CV34 5WE
England
Tel. 01926 499 619
Email: info@helion.co.uk
Website: www.helion.co.uk
Twitter: @helionbooks
Visit our blog at blog.helion.co.uk

Published by Helion & Company 2021
Designed and typeset by Mary Woolley (www.battlefield-design.co.uk)
Cover designed by Paul Hewitt, Battlefield Design (www.battlefield-design.co.uk)

ISBN 978-1-914059-26-1

British Library Cataloguing-in-Publication Data.
A catalogue record for this book is available from the British Library.

For details of other military history titles published by Helion & Company Limited contact the above address or visit our website: http://www.helion.co.uk.

We always welcome receiving book proposals from prospective authors.

Contents

Introduction 6

Part I: The Portuguese Two "Armies" 15
- War of the Two Brothers Portuguese Army 15
- Portuguese Uniforms, Arms and Equipment, 1815-34 16
- Liberal Army 37
- Miguelite Army 48
- Naval Forces 55

Part II: The War of the Two Brothers: Timeline of a Civil War 64
- Revolution of 24 August 1820 and Path to War 64
- First Absolutist Reactions Against the Liberals 66
- First Shots of the Civil War 67
- The Azores goes Liberal 69
- Siege of Porto 70
- A Bold Move: Liberal Expedition to Algarve 87
- Liberal Success in the South – Battle of Cape St. Vincent and Terceira's Advance through Alentejo 88
- Liberal Army on Two Fronts – Conquest of Lisbon and the end of the Siege of Porto 91
- The War of the Two Brothers in Southern Portugal 94
- The Miguelite Army still had claws 95
- Liberals and Miguelites Clash in Ribatejo 99
- Northern Front 102
- Battle of Asseiceira and War's End 104
- Aftermath 107

Bibliography 109

Introduction

This volume chronicles the Portuguese Civil War of 1828-34, commonly known in Anglophone sources as the Miguelite Wars or the War of the Two Brothers. It was an important moment in the European Liberal movement, prior to the Carlist Wars in Spain, and related to the revolutionary period of 1830 in France, and the 1848 revolutions throughout Europe, including the second Portuguese Civil War of 1846-47.

When the French invaded Portugal in 1807, Prince Regent of Portugal D. João withdraw with his family and court to Brazil. For the first time in his life he found happiness. He and his eldest son Pedro loved Brazil, while his wife and D. Miguel hated it. Even after the French had been banished from Portuguese territory, D. João refused to return – he simply preferred Brazil, and the Brazilians learned what it was like to have a government of their own. In theory Portugal was ruled by regents – however, in practice, it was run by Marshal Beresford, the authoritarian British officer who had initially been brought in to do no more than reorganize the Portuguese army. When popular discontentment and an uprising within the army unseated Beresford in 1820, King D. João VI finally agreed, most reluctantly, to return to Portugal. There he found a chaotic situation where Liberals, Ultra-Liberals, and absolutists vied for power. In 1823, D. Miguel, egged on by his mother, attempted to unseat his father and was subsequently exiled. Pedro, left in Brazil as regent for his father, declared independence in 1821 with himself as Emperor, renouncing his claim to the Portuguese throne.

King D. João VI by Fantan, Paris 1825. (National Library of Portugal)

When King João VI died, Pedro did his best to sort out the situation, granting a mildly Liberal constitution to Portugal and arranging for his nine-year-old daughter Maria to become Queen, with one of his sisters and D. Miguel as regent. D. Miguel betrayed his trust; upon his return to Portugal from exile, he tore up the constitution and declared himself King with his mother's backing. His mother demanded heads be cut off and hundreds were then executed, killed out of hand or by neglect, and thousands of Liberals filled the kingdom prisons in what became an absolutist reign of terror with the full support of the Church. Portugal entered a repressive dark age, dominated by an almost medieval religious intolerance, as the priests raised up the peasantry with a hatred of everything that the Catholic and aristocratic hierarchy hated – freemasons, Jews, Liberals, foreigners (especially the English) and Protestants. Liberals left for Brazil, France, Britain, and Spain, and there seemed to be precious little hope for Dona Maria. France was ruled by the last and most hard-headed of the Bourbons, Charles X, and Britain was under the reactionary Tory government of Wellington, while Spain languished under the dunder-headed rule of Fernando VII. At this time, D. Pedro was having problems of his own in Brazil.

Queen Carlota Joaquina. (National Library of Portugal)

The processes that would unleash the civil war in Portugal of 1828-34 had their roots in the Liberal movement of the 24th of August 1820. It was motivated by the discontentment of Portuguese military officers. They had been superseded by the British in the ranks of the Portuguese Army, along with the subordination of Portugal to England, almost as a protectorate. The idea of a written Constitution circumscribing the rights and duties of the citizen and the state was also being sought after with this movement. This action was inspired by the proclamation of the Spanish Constitution of Cadiz in 1813. The Constitution in Portugal was finally drafted and imposed between 1820-22. This was the embryo of the conflict between those whose intention was to propel Portugal up to the modernity of Great Britain, France, or a newly born Belgium, and those who'd rather have Portugal remain an absolutist and traditional kingdom. Upon the death of D. João VI, the individuals who would partake in the conflict emerged: on one side stood D. Pedro, Duke of Bragança, Prince Royal and Emperor of Brazil since 1822, and on the other, his younger brother, Prince D. Miguel, who, after the uprisings of the 27 May 1823 (Vilafrancada) and the 30 April 1824, had been exiled by his father, King D. João VI, to Austria. He would only return in 1828 to take the power by force, while relying on an increasingly conservative society, which feared the Liberals, 'Franc-Masons' and 'Jacobins' movements.[1] The succession question then became pertinent since D. Pedro, despite being Prince Royal and the legitimate successor to the throne, was also the Emperor of Brazil and would, therefore, simply not be able to reign in Lisbon, thus making it impossible for him to hold both crowns. This issue was brought to light most enthusiastically by his younger brother, Prince and Infante D. Miguel, with clear aspirations to the throne, which was being manipulated by his mother, Queen Carlota Joaquina, a Spanish woman characterized as irascible and devoutly absolutist.

The first attempt to solve the problem came from D. Pedro himself, who, on 26 April 1826, imposed the temporary regency of the Infanta D. Isabel Maria, his sister, and three days later on the 29 granted the Constitutional Charter (more conciliatory and less radical than the Constitution of 1822, the King being made to give away more powers to the parliament). On the 22 May of the same year, D. Pedro gave up the Crown of Portugal in favour of his eldest daughter, D. Maria da Gloria, then seven years old, whose hand in marriage had been promised to Prince D. Miguel, her uncle, after swearing to comply with

1 The Franc Masons and Jacobins were the terms used to refer the Portuguese Masonic movements and lodges.

D. Pedro de Bragança, Emperor of Brazil, King of Portugal and Regent of His Daughter Dona Maria II. (National Library of Portugal)

the Constitutional Charter. Once married, D. Miguel could take over the Kingdom. This was a moderating solution that potentially pleased everyone, bridging the growing gap between Liberals and absolutists.

The conflict between Liberals and Absolutists was part of an international context that had been triggered in France back in 1789, and in which the eminently bourgeois Liberal currents faced the collapsing world that European absolutism had summoned. In neighbouring Spain, the counterparts of the Portuguese parties in conflict, who were each supporting their corresponding sides, ended up getting involved as well.

D. Carlota Joaquina had been planting intrigues behind the scenes, triggering military revolts led by absolutist officers, her loyal followers. They were then pursued by government troops and fled to Spain, where they would be given support, including artillery, to reinforce the offensive power of a future absolutist invasion. Spanish support, however, did not prevent two attempts at absolutist invasion from failing.

Faced with the threat, the Lisbon government appealed to England, requesting military aid to government reinforced the capitol's garrison against the absolutist rebels, resulting in the British promptly landing in Portugal. The British government took the initiative and promoted D. Miguel and acceptance of the Constitutional Charter. The British Embassy agreed to allow the Royal Marines from Royal Navy ships in the Tagus to land in Lisbon invoking the protection of the Portuguese royal family. The situation became more unstable in the last week of November 1826 when 2,200 armed Miguelite rebels, coming from Spain, entered Portugal. The British government, with the Parliament approval finally dispatched 5,000 British troops, namely of Line Infantry and Light Infantry Regiments, Light Dragoons, and Royal Marines, to Portugal to face down the threat of Miguelite deserters from the Portuguese Army, and any new insurgents, coming from Spain which was sheltering the Miguelite supporters. Organizing General Clinton's force demonstrated the demanding measures needed to assemble that relatively small contingent to operate in Europe and not in a colonial operation. The first contingent of 2,813 men arrived in five ships between 27–31 December 1826. The Miguelite insurgents were active in the north-east, having taken the frontier fortress of Almeida and having occupied Vizeu, a strategic point and Guarda near the Spanish border. The rebel forces included discharged veterans, disloyal regiments, and peasants, led by disaffected Miguelite officers sometimes banded together. The British expeditionary force reached nearly 5,400 rank and file by the third week of January 1827. In addition, four Royal Navy warships supplied 242 marines to occupy two key forts on the Tagus River estuary. Advancing inland, British troops had advanced to Alenquer and Cartaxo, and to Leiria, about 100 kilometres from Lisbon's centre, by early February. By 24 February, some 1,900 British troops were based in Coimbra, about halfway between Lisbon and the northern border with Spain. Once the threat of civil war passed, the British government faced the choice of withdrawing the British Army or keeping it in Portugal until stability was established.[2] On 31 July 1827, in the Royal Palace of Ajuda, Lisbon, the government and aristocracy swore to comply with the Constitutional Charter and on 4 October of the same year, in Vienna, D. Miguel swore to do the same. Carlota Joaquina's absolutist party, however, were preparing the coup that would return power to absolutism, undermining the foundations of the current Liberal regime.

Royal Prince and later King D. Miguel I (Portrait by Johann Nepomuk Ender).

The whole process was rushed with the return of D. Miguel who was acclaimed absolute King in Lisbon on 22 February 1828. It was a real *coup d'etat* when the absolutists (or Miguelites) invaded the Ajuda Palace and forced everyone there to acclaim the absolutist regime at bayonet point. It was the preponderance of the old traditional values in a mostly illiterate and clergy-dominated popular stratum that did not forgive D. Pedro's actions in defence of Brazil's independence. As soon as D. Miguel took over as regent in late February 1828, the British expeditionary force received orders to leave Portugal from 11 March 1828, leaving the weakened Liberal faction unprotected. The path for the civil war was now clearly open.

With the arrival of D. Miguel began the ruthless persecution of the Liberals. In Lisbon, gangs of rogues insulted and beat up suspected Liberals or Franc Masons. The state's means of oppression were multiplied, and the military corps created in the previous regime, such as the Corps of Commerce Volunteers, National Artillery and Infantry Battalions in Lisbon, and D. Pedro IV and D. Maria II Volunteers in Porto, were all dissolved. The Liberal government structures were eliminated, extinguishing the House of Representatives. In fact, this uncontrolled and destructive euphoria was unavoidably triggering unrest in the European powers, notably in Great Britain, France and Austria, the latter nation being where Prince Metternich (Prime Minister) was realizing that D. Miguel had not followed his advice for restraint and prudence. Spain was the only country supportive of D. Miguel. Hatred and revenge began to spread all over Portugal, where some private *vendettas* were taken under political pretexts.

D. Miguel's political intent was to internally legitimize the absolutist regime, while the Liberals or even moderate conservatives in Portugal went underground and only managed to protest in clandestine movements, often ending in the scaffold, especially between March 1828 and August 1831. Often these conflicts were taken into the Special Tribunals and consequently ended with prison or the gallows. Prisons and forts such as S. Julião da Barra were filled with Liberals, and espionage, informants, and violence were

2 B. Collins, 'The Limits of British Power: Intervention in Portugal, 1820–30', *The International History Review*, 35:4 (2013), 744-765, DOI: 10.1080/07075332.2013.813567, pp. 752-758.

frequent. The exiled Liberals, all over Europe, heartened to see the 1830 Liberal movements in France and Belgium, publish newspapers, prints, and pamphlets about D. Miguel's usurpation of power. Also, on the other side, even long academic theses were printed that aimed to justify D. Miguel's actions against D. Pedro and the Liberals. The Liberal reactions against D. Miguel intensified as he implemented absolutism through an increasingly dictatorship-like regime, triggering military conspiracies and revolts between March and April 1828 in Lisbon garrison regiments. Then the clashes spread to Aveiro, Coimbra, Faro, and Porto, where a Liberal Government Board arose, but failed before the prompt response of the already "converted-to-Miguelite" Army. The Liberals who wanted to survive turned into a wave of emigrants in 1828. Their numbers included several notable characters such as José Ferreira Borges, José da Silva Carvalho, Almeida Garrett, and others who fled to England. Agostinho José Freire, Bernardo de Sá Nogueira (future Marquis of Sá da Bandeira), Domingos António Sequeira etc. moved to France. The lives of some of these exiled men were relatively good depending on the aid and conditions of asylum, but many felt that they should demand better conditions or received support from Portuguese traders living abroad.

The episode of the steamship *Belfast* in May 1828 contributed to the origin of two Liberal factions, as there were differences between the ideas of two major characters in Portuguese Liberalism – Saldanha and Palmela. Then emerged two groups: the *Saldanhistas* and the *Palmelistas*. After this episode and its failed military pronouncement, the Liberal contingent besieged and pursued by the powerful Miguelite army, withdrew to Galicia, where it would suffer traumatic experiences. Many Liberals later travelled in groups to England, such as the Academic Volunteer Corps, joining Palmela and Candido José Xavier, and living under harsh conditions as well. In the meantime, Saldanha and his group in Paris got the support of the French Government in 1829 to prepare a first naval expedition to Terceira Island in the Azores archipelago, which ultimately failed due to the British fleet there barring the coming expedition.

The 'Portuguese question' was fervently followed and discussed in the European press and by European governments in 1828-29. An important factor was the arrival of D. Pedro in Europe, now only Duke of Bragança after having passed down the throne of Brazil and Portugal to his children. From England, still in 1829, also sailed a contingent of emigrants that would help the Liberal nucleus under siege at Angra Castle, on Terceira Island. Meanwhile, in November 1830, Wellington, a resolute Tory who was in the process of recognizing D. Miguel's government, resigned as Prime minister of the British Government, and was replaced by the Whigs led by the second Earl Grey. This political shift proved beneficial to the Liberal effort; it was then possible to provide new manpower and logistical resources, strengthening the military assets of the of the Count of Vila-Flor (future Duke of Terceira). This enabled the occupation of the remaining Azores archipelago.

Count of Vila Flor and Duke of Terceira.
(National Library of Portugal)

The foundations were underway for the preparation of the military expedition to the continent, although this process proved difficult and costly, forcing loans, hiring mercenaries, acquiring weapons and forming a small assault navy squadron. Once organized in the ports of Brittany, the Liberal expedition sailed on the 10 February 1832 from the port of Belle-Isle towards the Azorean archipelago. Upon his arrival on Terceira Island on 3 March 1832, D. Pedro proclaimed himself regent in the name of Queen D. Maria II, his eldest daughter, forming the Liberal government. The legislative and administrative reforms carried out by its Finance Minister, José Xavier Mouzinho da Silveira, were also of the utmost importance. After the necessary preparations for the Liberal expedition were concluded, this small army set sail to Portugal.

D. Pedro's squadron was headed by Admiral Rose Sartorius and consisted of 50 ships carrying about 8,300 men (Portuguese sources refers 7,500 men). The landing took place north of Porto, on 8 July 1832, at Arnosa de Pampelido beach, near Mindelo. There was no resistance from the Miguelite troops, and the reason why the garrison commander, Viscount Santa Marta, withdrew from Porto to the south bank of the Douro is still unknown. The Liberal army then went on forced marches to Porto with the 5th Caçadores Battalion scouting ahead and ended up entering the city the next morning, but without the enthusiastic adhesion that D. Pedro expected. Meanwhile, the government formed on Terceira Island returns to its role in Porto, continuing its legislative action and seeking funding to support the war.

The occupation of Porto by D. Pedro came as a surprise to D. Miguel, who was convinced the Liberal landing was to take place in Lisbon. The Miguelite General, Póvoas, was therefore sent to General Viscount Santa Marta's aid with four well-equipped brigades, later reinforced to three divisions and a mobile brigade. The small Liberal army was facing the possibility of battling against a huge army of 80,000 men including first-line troops, militias, Ordenança brigades, Royalist volunteers, and numerous guerrilla bands.

In the Liberal field, two theses emerged for what the optimal approach for combat would be: an offensive attitude advocated by the Count of Vila-Flor and a defensive method suggested by the veteran and hardened General Bernardo de Sá Nogueira.

Initially, the Liberal army made offensive attacks towards the north, namely Guimarães and Braga. It made reconnaissance advances to the east, in Penafiel and Valongo, clashing with strong Miguelite contingents at Ponte Ferreira and Souto Redondo. Despite having come out victorious in the first instance they were seriously defeated in the second location and withdrew to Porto. D. Pedro was forced to barricade himself in the city, leaving a detachment in the Convent of Serra of Pilar, on the south bank of the river Douro thus, controlling that point of the river and causing the dispersal of the Miguelite forces.

Admiral Sir George Rose Sartorius. (National Library of Portugal)

Bernardo de Sá Nogueira, Viscount and Marquis of Sá da Bandeira. (National Library of Portugal)

The siege of Porto lasted about a year, pushing the city to fortify itself, building defence lines supported by batteries, forts or strongholds that, despite being improvised and having required constant maintenance, withstood the Miguelite offensives, such as those of 29 September 1832 and 25 July 1833, among many other battles, combats or small skirmishing clashes. However, the situation during the siege became complicated: with hunger, epidemics, desertions, late payment of soldiers, and riots at the police station. Attempts at settlement and negotiations failed because of the irreducible positions taken by the contenders.

Throughout June and July, the Miguelites concentrated troops for the final assault, which took place on the 25 July 1833 under Bourmont's command. In a bold initiative, the Count of Vila-Flor, with a force of 2,500 men and a small Navy squadron under the command of Admiral Charles Napier, set sail for the Algarve to ease the pressure on Porto.[3] The landing of the Count of Vila-Flor and his troops took place on 24 June 1833, near the town of Monte Gordo, with no significant resistance. In the Algarve, Admiral Napier's squadron delivered a heavy defeat on the Miguelite naval fleet in a battle near Cape St. Vincent.

These successes in the south of the country raised the morale of the Liberals and seriously undermined the convictions of many Miguelites, leading them to abandon their cause. The Count of Vila-Flor, now Duke of Terceira, advanced through the Alentejo, crossing this province towards Lisbon with Napier's naval support. He entered an abandoned Lisbon on 24 July 1833 on the eve of the victory of Bourmont and his army over the Liberal garrison of Porto. The last Miguelite obstacle before Lisbon, General Teles Jordão and his division, had been defeated in Almada by the Duke of Terceira's forces.

D. Pedro then left Porto to form a government as regent in Lisbon and, almost simultaneously, D. Miguel left his headquarters in Braga, also heading to the capital to reoccupy it and expel the Liberals. But upon arriving near Lisbon, he realized that the capital was already in Liberal hands and was being strongly defended with fortifications much like the ones in Porto. D. Miguel was forced to remain and establish his HQ in Santarém.

3 'Sir Charles Napier, Count Napier de São Vicente, (born 6 March 1786, near Falkirk, Stirling, Scotland , died November 6, 1860, near Catherington, Hampshire, England), admiral in the Portuguese and British navies, the controversial commander of the British Baltic Fleet during the Crimean War of 1853-56. Created Conde Napier de São Vicente in the Portuguese peerage, he was less elegantly known in Great Britain as "Black Charley" and "Mad Charley." *Encyclopaedia Britannica* «https://www.britannica.com/biography/Sir-Charles-Napier-Conde-Napier-de-Sao-Vicente» (accessed 22 Aug. 2020).

The charismatic Liberal Marshal, João Carlos de Saldanha Oliveira e Daun, Duke of Saldanha, in turn caused the remaining Miguelite troops to lift the siege of the city of Porto and then went to the south to surround Santarém. His campaign was brilliant, as he conquered Leiria and Torres Novas, defeated the Miguelites in Pernes and in Almoster, all between January and February 1834.

Another key figure in the Liberal Army, Bernardo de Sá Nogueira (Baron of Sá da Bandeira), went to the Algarve to control the Miguelite guerrilla, which he did, and then advanced to Baixo Alentejo where, in S. Bartolomeu de Messines he had to retreat before the troops of the Miguelite Brigadier Cabreira supported by large parties of guerrilla bands.

Marshal and Marquis de Saldanha. (National Library of Portugal)

The celebrated General Silva Torres, defender of Serra of Pilar, successfully occupied the province of Minho, despite the fierce resistance of Miguelite forces still having hold of cities like Braga or Guimarães. Once again, the Duke of Terceira went into action and, between April and May, took control of the Trás-os-Montes and Beiras provinces, because of the many popular movements that were ready to acclaim the constitutional cause there. The Marshal will still triumph in the battle of Asseiceira, and by pushing out the Miguelist troops, managed to make his way to Santarém, leading D. Miguel to retreat to Évora either to offer resistance or to take refuge in neighbouring Spain.

It was the final blow to D. Miguel's absolutist regime, in a time when Spain was already embroiled in a civil war between Liberals and the D. Carlos absolutists. The Iberian situation shook up Europe's governments, Liberal or Conservative; this worried England and France since they had old connections to Portugal and Spain respectively. So, an alliance between these four countries was created in order to support the rise of Liberal regimes both in Portugal and Spain and the exile of D. Miguel and D. Carlos de España is foreseen.

It was because of this that General Rodil and two Spanish divisions crossed the border of Beira in pursuit of D. Carlos who had fled to Évora where D. Miguel was. The actions of this Spanish contingent relieved the pressure in the centre of Portugal and thus the army under the command of the Duke of Terceira marched to the Alentejo to deliver the *coup de grace* on the remainder of the weakened army of D. Miguel that had no more than 10, 500 men at that point, many of them ready to desert.

From this perspective, the officers of D. Miguel's staff, in council, made the final decision to surrender and sign an armistice. This was signed in Évora-Monte in the presence of General Lemos by D. Miguel, and Saldanha and Terceira by D. Pedro. This resulted in a truly indulgent amnesty for a large majority of D. Miguel's followers. This led to widespread rejection by many Liberals in Portugal until D. Pedro death. However, D. Miguel was exiled *ad eternum*, taking with him an annual appropriation of a substantial allowance and possession of his own property. But later he lost these favours because he never renounced his claims to the throne until his death in Vienna in 1866. Then and there did the bloodiest struggle for the survival of Portuguese Liberalism and the end of an absolutist system typical of the Old Regime reach a final conclusion.

Part I

The Portuguese Two "Armies"

War of the Two Brothers Portuguese Army

In 1806 a new uniform plan was created. Perfectly adapted to the military fashions of Europe, the obsolete tricorne, the old pantaloons by the knee and other old fashioned items were replaced by the shako (Barretina) and by a simplified and sober uniform consisting of a short-tailed coat of dark Prussian blue (Azul Ferrete), now closed by the waist, and trousers, divided into winter model in blue cloth, and the summer model in linen fabric. The first type of trousers or pantaloons were tightened by the ankle and complemented with thick black cloth gaiters on the trousers and shoe. The second type was made of white linen and its clipping was unusual since it was tightened in its lower part by a similar flap to a gaiter that tightened between the heel and the sole of the shoe. The infantry, artillery, and cavalry line regiments were now differentiated only by the colour combinations on the collars, the cuffs and the piping's of the coats. Turning to the regiment, the light, fusilier, and grenadier companies were differentiated by the aigrettes or tufts of the shakos: green for the light company, white for the fusiliers and red for the grenadier companies. The uniforms of the militia regiments, the second line of defence of the kingdom, were similar to those of the line troops, and following the distinctive method of the first line, although the buttons, yellow in the line regiments, were of white metal for the militia units, and the shakos had the name of the town where the men were raised, instead of the regimental number. The third line, constituted by the Ordenanças brigades,[1] of a strongly rural nature and a militia organization, had more peculiar uniforms based on coarse brown fabrics such as the *Burel* or *Saragoça*, although the Ordenança officers wore green long-tailed coats. During the Peninsular War in 1809, the light infantry was finally converted into the Caçadores battalions, initially with six units and, from 1811, expanding to twelve battalions, assuming for many years the character of elite troops; they were greatly appreciated by the British high command during the Peninsular War. The light infantry Caçadores were characterized by their brown uniforms, usually from the Saragoça fabric intended for sergeants and ranks and in better wool fabrics for the officers. Undoubtedly based in design on the British green-clad riflemen of the 95th and 60th Rifles regiments or the King's German Legion, the Caçadores, whose combat technique was carried out in scattered order and using the experience of snipers

1 The Ordenanças were a third line or reserve troops, created in the 16th century and extinguished in 1834. The first line were the regular units of the Army, then the Militia Regiments and at last the Ordenança Companies and Brigades. These troops were mainly a recruitment reserve for the Militia and Line units of the Portuguese Army and could not be deployed as front line units, although they were very useful in irregular operations and sieges.

with selective targets, needed uniforms that disguised them in the landscape, avoiding their detection by the enemy.

Still in the context of the Peninsular War, the Portuguese cavalry and artillery were also clad in Prussian blue, albeit with characteristic uniforms decreed by the uniform Plan of 1806, consisting of the short uniform, short breeches, high black leather boots and a leather helmet, very much like the British Tarleton, adorned with horse mane crest. The regimental differentiations were made as in the infantry.

Despite the extensive reorganization carried out by Wellington and Beresford, the uniforms of the Portuguese army maintained their basic cut until the Civil War of 1828-34, undergoing small modifications in 1815, not long after the end of the Peninsular War.

Portuguese Uniforms, Arms and Equipment, 1815-34

The Portuguese Civil War, also known as the Miguelite Wars or the War of Two Brothers has a range of military uniforms both from the Portuguese Miguelite and Liberal Army. As for the foreign troops, the last ones mostly volunteers that cannot be understood without addressing at least the Uniform Plan of 1806-10 and the regulations of 1815, since the new plan that followed was only published after the Civil War in 1834. Through the 1815-34 period, there were certainly several changes in the Portuguese uniforms, not to mention the troubled period from 1832 to 1834, through the War of Two Brothers or Miguelite Wars, especially in what concerns the volunteer corps from both sides.

One of the major problems with this period is the lack of reliable and contemporary iconography, regulations, and sources. The 1815 plan did not have a full sequence of illustrations that should have accompanied it. Some loose engravings might be illustrative of this plan, but nothing can prove it, in fact, this whole period lives much on the assumption of 'maybe' or 'could be.' To make matters more complicated, it is not even known for sure whether the 1815 Plan was published (printed) or if it was ever even fully applied until the 1834 Uniform Plan. This could have been an attempt to regulate what was already dispersed in the Orders of the Day and the separate legislation, especially since the end of the Peninsular War.

As an example of the doubts above, we can look at the Infantry shakos, the format of which the 1815 plan does not explain, stating that '... all the most officers, junior officers and soldiers, etc.' By deducing that they are of equal model, the only exception is that '...officers may wear all hats made as approved.' However, in iconographic engravings and other sources, officers and sergeants appear with a bell-topped shako model, and the ranks with the model very similar to the old model English stovepipe shako, but an 1817 a General Staff note says that '... the shape and strings of shakos should be retained as they are now used.'The Ordinance of 19 October 1815 appears to have been the last army regulation Army until the 1834 Uniform Plan.

What follows below broadly chronicles the Portuguese Army of 1815-32, During this period it was divided in two opposing forces, the Liberal Army of D. Pedro and the Miguelite Army, under the supreme commander of D. Miguel, the former's younger brother, hence the 'War of the Two Brothers'.

Infantry

From 1815 onwards, some engravings show that the ranks still used the old English style Stovepipe shako, while the NCOs and officers, up to the rank of colonel, wore the new bell-topped shakos. The old flat rank epaulettes were replaced by grenadier style wings. All the previous accoutrements were of Peninsular War vintage retained as durable materials, as in other armies, since the combat equipment relied on the use of the ubiquitous Brown Bess India pattern musket with flintlock system, a model supplied to Portugal

Peninsular War Portuguese Infantry. (Sérgio Veludo Coelho)

during the Peninsular War and onwards, including the shorter Light Infantry Musket, both for the Light companies of the Infantry Regiments and the Caçadores Battalions, the latter also with the Baker rifle.

Another adopted style from the British reorganization was the habit of having the trousers, or pantaloons, over the gaiters, the latter in thick black canvas or wool. In reality, except for what we may consider small details, in 1832, at the beginning of the large scale operations of the Miguelite Wars, the Portuguese Army infantry regiments were mostly dressed and equipped within the standards of the 1806 Uniform Plan and the 1810-14 field changes of the British reorganization under Marshal William Beresford.

This could also apply for the rest of the Portuguese Army, considering the regular units of Cavalry, Artillery, and the Engineers. Even the Militia Regiments followed this standard. The volunteer units would be different in many ways, mostly through foreign mercenaries' influence. This was the situation both for the Liberal and the Miguelite Regiments, similar in appearance, different only in the regulation facings of the uniforms. This was after all a civil war. The facings and equipment of the largest Portuguese corps, the infantry, were as follows:

Portuguese Line Infantry Regiments facings 1815-34

1815 1834	Coat	Collar	Cuffs	Piping	Summer Trouser	Winter Trouser	Gaiters	Accoutrements
nº 1	Blue	Blue	White	White	White	Blue	Black	White
nº 2	Blue	Blue	White	Scarlet	White	Blue	Black	White
nº3	Blue	Blue	White	Yellow	White	Blue	Black	White
nº 4	Blue	Blue	Scarlet	White	White	Blue	Black	White
nº 5	Blue	Blue	Scarlet	Scarlet	White	Blue	Black	White
nº 6	Blue	Blue	Scarlet	Yellow	White	Blue	Black	White
nº 7	Blue	Blue	Yellow	White	White	Blue	Black	White
nº 8	Blue	Blue	Yellow	Scarlet	White	Blue	Black	White
nº 9	Blue	Blue	Yellow	Yellow	White	Blue	Black	White
nº 10	Blue	Blue	Light Blue	White	White	Blue	Black	White
nº 11	Blue	Blue	Light Blue	Scarlet	White	Blue	Black	White
nº 12	Blue	Blue	Light Blue	Yellow	White	Blue	Black	White
nº 13	Blue	White	White	White	White	Blue	Black	White
nº 14	Blue	White	White	White	White	Blue	Black	White
nº 15	Blue	White	White	Yellow	White	Blue	Black	White
nº 16	Blue	Scarlet	Scarlet	White	White	Blue	Black	White
nº 17	Blue	Scarlet	Scarlet	Scarlet	White	Blue	Black	White
nº 18	Blue	Scarlet	Scarlet	Yellow	White	Blue	Black	White
nº 19	Blue	Yellow	Yellow	White	White	Blue	Black	White
nº 20	Blue	Yellow	Yellow	Scarlet	White	Blue	Black	White
nº 21	Blue	Yellow	Yellow	Yellow	White	Blue	Black	White
nº 22	Blue	Light Blue	Light Blue	White	White	Blue	Black	White
nº 23	Blue	Light Blue	Light Blue	Scarlet	White	Blue	Black	White
nº 24	Blue	Light Blue	Light Blue	Yellow	White	Blue	Black	White

Officers

Bell-topped Shako

Made of leather and felt with a tin flap except for the top and the flap, varnished, and lined by the outside of black cloth. They would have had an iron rim inside the top and the plates were the same as those in the 1806 model until 1832, when the Liberal troops adopted the new shako plates of Queen Dona Maria II. They used a lace of gold around the top. The officers could use velveteen or velvet to cover the shako, instead of the regulation black cloth. The chin strap was of brass scales.

Ranks

Stovepipe Shako

Made of leather and thick card frame with a black leather flap and covered on the outside in black cloth. The shako plates were the same as the ones in the 1806 model until 1832, when the Liberal troops adopted new shako plates. There were no chin straps, the shako relying on a perfect fit over the soldier's head.

All Ranks

Coat and trousers

From 1764 to 1834, the Portuguese Army basic colour Infantry uniforms were dark blue (also known as Prussian blue) and became progressively more like British uniforms in cut and design as Britain's involvement became more and more extensive between 1809-15; shoulder wings were employed, also in blue and white cloth and fringes. Grenadier companies were scarlet.

As with their British equivalents, the coat had a relatively short cut, except for generals and specialized army services like the Royal Arsenal, whose coats had long tails. The leather cross belts and slings were white, and the shako was of a 'stovepipe' design. The officers had gold fringed metal epaulettes, but the new 1815 regulations abolished the old 1806 gold fringe and cord code for officers and replaced them with combinations of golden laces and cords, introducing the ranks in golden laces above the cuffs. The NCOs had similar epaulettes, but the fringes were in silk cord, and from 1815 the sergeant's grades were in the British style, using yellow silk chevrons according to each rank or black for the light infantry. The 1815 regulations for the trousers or pantaloons were, for the winter model, in Prussian blue cloth, and for the summer, white linen or canvas, always covering the black cloth gaiters. The shoes were made from black leather.

Vest

Of blue wool cloth with sleeves, usually called police coats, quite similar to the British shell jackets.

Overcoat

Of grey blend thick woollen cloth.

Armament

Since the Peninsular War, the Portuguese line infantry had been fully armed with English Brown Bess flintlock muskets, mostly India Pattern, and, after 1815, with the new Land Light Infantry Pattern. Equipment consisted of two cross belts: one from which a black leather cartridge pouch hung, while the other belt supported the bayonet. However, with the British assistance programme, some equipment, all black leather, was distributed to the troops. With the Civil War and the division of the Portuguese Army, the

Miguelites and the Liberals both employed the weapons described above, whilst the latter also purchased French flintlock muskets of Napoleonic vintage like the Année IX and the more modern 1821 models. Also, in English and Belgian sources, the importation of Belgian flintlocks is mentioned, probably the newly made 1831 model, and that may have been the rifled version, but there is not a reliable confirmation of this. In the Miguelite forces, the English weaponry continued to be used, or Portuguese copies made in the Army Royal Arsenal, namely the India Pattern musket with socket bayonet and the already mentioned Light Infantry version with the sword bayonet similar to the one on the Caçadores Baker Rifles.

Ranks
Officers
Generals and Brigadiers
Golden stars in the epaulette upper flat – one for Brigadier, two for General.
Colonel
Two laces of gold round and one of gold cord each of the sleeve cuffs
Lieutenant Colonel
Two laces of gold round each of the sleeve cuffs
Major
Like the previous one but only with a lace and a gold cord parallel to it.
Captain
Like the previous but without cord
Lieutenant
Two golden cords around each cuff
Ensign
A gold cord.
Note: Companies officers have a yellow metal whistle attached to the uniform on the left side employing a cord of the same metal.
Non-Commissioned Officers
Assistant Sergeant
Four golden lace chevrons, placed on the right arm and nailed to the seams of the sleeve, with the apex facing the elbow side and a yellow metal crown in the centre of the last chevron that is to the side of the shoulder.
Quarter Master Sergeant
The same badges as the previous one but placed on the left arm.
First Sergeant
Four golden lace chevrons on the right arm.
Second Sergeant
Three chevrons
Junior Sergeant

Same as above but on the left arm
Chief Trumpet
Same as the second sergeant.
Corporal
Two chevrons of yellow wool on the right arm
Lance Corporal
A single chevron of yellow wool on the right arm
Sapper
Two axes of yellow cloth placed in quotation marks on his right arm about halfway from elbow to shoulder.
Grenadiers Company
Prussian-blue epaulets with the of the Piping of the uniform, catching all the shoulder just under the sleeve; white fringe.

Light Infantry/Caçadores

The Portuguese Caçadores, especially during the Peninsular War and civil wars period, became a well-known military corps, mostly after Wellington's and Beresford's reorganization of the Portuguese army which was disbanded by the first French invasion of Portugal in 1808. With the presence of the British Army in Portuguese territory and the French threat not far from the border, Wellington and the Portuguese government ordered a hurried reorganization of the Portuguese army including the creation of six Caçadores battalions. The Caçadores were created by a Royal decree of 14 October 1808, but only on the 15 December was the order given to raise the battalions. The 1st, 2nd and 4th battalions were raised in the border provinces of Beira and Alentejo, the 3rd and the 5th in the Trás-os-Montes province and the 6th battalion in the Minho province, mostly along the border with Spain. The majority of Portuguese Caçadores were men of the mountains or farmers, with hunting habits and experience in using guns individually. This enabled them to handle Baker rifles with deadly proficiency. Like many other European units of the same category, the Portuguese Caçadores were supposed to outflank enemy positions and harass select targets.

By the decree of the 14 October 1808, the basic structure of a Caçadores battalion was composed of a staff corps and five companies of 123 men each. One of the battalion companies was raised as sharpshooters (*Atiradores*), very similar to the chosen men of the British rifles regiments and this meant that the Portuguese shooters were to be equipped with Baker rifles supplied by the British government. The other four companies still used smoothbore muskets, either Portuguese or British India Land pattern Brown Bess models.

Caçadores battalion components from 1808-34 were as follows:

Command and Staff
1 Lieutenant Colonel
1 Major
1 Adjutant
1 Quartermaster
1 Chaplain
1 Surgeon
2 Surgeon assistants
1 Gunsmith for the wood works
1 Gunsmith for the iron works
1 Master drummer
2 Buglers
Total: 13 men
Caçadores/Sharpshooter Company
1 Captain
1 Lieutenant
2 Ensigns (Alferes)
1 First Sargent
2 Second Sergeants
1 Junior Sergeant (Furriel)
8 Corporals
8 Lance corporals
2 Drummers
1 Bugler
96 Soldiers
total: 123 men
Total
Command – 13 men
4 Caçadores companies – 492 men (with India Pattern or Light Infantry Patterns)
1 Sharpshooter company- 123 men (with Baker Rifles)
Total: 628 men.

This composition was maintained after the 1809-11 Portuguese Army reorganization and the raising of six more Caçadores battalions in May 1811. These units reinforced the Anglo-Portuguese Army with reliable shock troops, who should be able to fight in the difficult terrains of Portugal and Spain.

Caçadores Battalions facings:

1815 1834	Coat	Collar	Cuffs	Piping	Summer Trouser	Winter Trouser	Gaiters	Accoutrements
nº 1	Blue	Black	Light Blue	Black	White	Brown	Black	Black
nº 2	Blue	Black	Scarlet	Black	White	Brown	Black	Black
Nº3	Brown	Black	Black	Black	White	Brown	Black	Black
nº 4	Brown	Light Blue	Scarlet	Black	White	Brown	Black	Black
nº 5	Brown	Scarlet	Scarlet	Black	White	Brown	Black	Black
nº 6	Brown	Yellow	Yellow	Black	White	Brown	Black	Black
nº 7	Brown	Black	Yellow	Black	White	Brown	Black	Black
nº 8	Brown	Light Blue	Black	Black	White	Brown	Black	Black
nº 9	Brown	Scarlet	Yellow	Black	White	Brown	Black	Black
nº 10	Brown	Yellow	Black	Black	White	Brown	Black	Black
nº 11	Brown	Light Blue	Scarlet	Black	White	Brown	Black	Black
nº 12	Brown	Scarlet	Light Blue	Black	White	Brown	Black	Black

Officers

Bell-topped Shako

After 1815, the Caçadores officers partially adopted the bell-topped shako made of leather with a tin flap, except the top and the flap which were varnished and lined in black fabric on the outside. As with the line infantry, it also had a lace of gold around the top. The officers could use velveteen or velvet to cover the shako. The chin strap would be of brass scales. The battalion number was placed under a large brass bugle-horn badge with laurel leaves and the newer models had long green silk cords around the shako falling right just to the front buttons of the coat. The Caçadores' shakos had long black plumes, especially after 1820. However, many officers and NCOs retained stovepipe shakos and some engravings depict a model taller than the 1815 pattern. During the War of the Two Brothers, the Miguelite Caçadores are often shown in bell-topped shakos all ranks unlike the Liberal Army, which retained the stovepipe version.

Ranks

Stovepipe Shako

The Portuguese 1806 tall front shako was replaced in 1809 by the cheaper and simple black fabric stovepipe British shako. This was adopted throughout the Portuguese Army including the Caçadores battalions. As with the officers' and NCO shakos, the battalion number was placed under the bugle-horn badge and green cords were added in the same way as in the higher ranks. The green tuft for Caçadores companies and the black tuft for the sharpshooter's companies were top and front on the shako and just above a cockade and lace with the royal colours of the Bragança dynasty. Some models had a folding peak much like the English pattern Rifles shakos. The rank shakos were of leather and thick card frame with a black leather flap and lined on the outside in black cloth. There were no chin straps, the shako's secure attachment to the soldier's head relying on a perfect fit.

All Ranks

Coat and Trousers

The Caçadores uniforms were, from 1808 to the Civil War, manufactured in dark brown cloth, (known as *Saragoça*) which was worn by this corps to the 1880s. The 1808 Caçadores uniform had a wide yellow cord lace. This was typical for chasseur style troops. However, the yellow chest cords would be too visible and were changed to black in 1810-11 and remained that way until 1868. Since 1815 the shoulder straps were dark brown with distinctive black piping and fringing. The collars were quite tall, and the cuffs were pointed, being piped in black and the battalion colours.

Officers and NCOs had similar uniforms but with golden piping on the cords, collar, and cuffs for the former and silk for the latter. The officers also sported golden metal shoulder straps in cavalry style, and a scarlet sash with silver fringe. Instead of gaiters, officers usually wore tall black leather boots, cavalry style or even the more expensive Hessian models. In the winter, all the troops wore the dark brown pantaloons over the black cloth gaiters. In summertime, the units were permitted to wear white linen or cotton trousers over the gaiters.

By Army Order (*Ordem do Exército*) of 30 July 1811, all the Caçadores battalions continued to be distinguished by the colours of their collars and cuffs and the battalion number in the shako plate. However, the 1808 uniform was changed to a less visible design, coming even closer to the British Rifles style. Due to the almost destroyed Portuguese economic structure, many parts of the army uniforms were impossible to locally manufacture, so the British command ordered to import to Portugal a wide variety of military materials.

The evolution of the Caçadores uniforms during this period demonstrates a strong influence of the earlier Loyal Lusitanian Legion and the British 95th and 60th Rifle regiments, especially in the hussar styled short-tailed coat, with three rows of yellow, and later black bone buttons. Keeping the distinctive dark brown fabric, the coat had black cords and piped in the chest, the cuffs were also pointed with black piping. The old infantry cut shoulder straps were replaced by British style models with black wool tufts at the extremes of the straps, which were also black piped with the inner parts in dark brown. The dark brown pantaloons and the white trousers remained unchanged, but the old black gaiters were replaced by a shorter model with pointed tops. The black colour was maintained. Officers and NCOs also adopted the new uniform but kept the earlier rank distinctions from the 1808 model, the sergeants and corporals wearing black silk chevron rank badges. With the raising of the six new battalions in 1811, the systems of colours of the collars and cuffs were changed to a more complex combination and the brown collars of the 1st, 2nd, and 3rd battalions became black.

Vest

Of brown wool cloth with sleeves, usually called police coats, very similar to the British shell jackets.

Overcoat

Of grey blend thick woollen cloth.

Armament

Between 1808 and 1834, the main accoutrements of the Caçadores battalions were most certainly of British provenience, being the standard models for light infantry. The Caçadores only received Baker rifles in early 1810 despite the weapons having been ordered in June 1809. By this time, the use of smoothbore muskets like the Brown Bess or the Portuguese pattern, as with the new Land English muskets, was restricted. The early Caçadores were supposed to make surprise attacks or outflank enemy positions rather than aim at selected targets; it was nearly impossible to achieve such a thing with smoothbore muskets until the arrival of the Baker rifles.

When the Caçadores finally adopted the Baker rifled carbine, they became experts in its handling. The use of the Baker carbine also led to the adoption of the British Rifle black leather accoutrements, with main ammo box and powder horn for separate loadings, belly box with cartridges for quick loadings and the frog scabbard for the sword-bayonet. Baker rifles were not available to all Caçadores soldiers, the others keeping the smoothbore muskets and accoutrements. In 1811, there were 2,100 Baker rifles in twelve Caçadores battalions, which would be 150-200 rifles per battalion, still a most respectable total of riflemen in any contemporary army. The Caçadores officers first employed the Portuguese 1806 pattern sword with a curved blade, but many later adopted the better quality British 1796 light cavalry sword, with a curved blade as well, lasting until the Miguelite Wars and standard issue for both armies. The sword and scabbard were suspended by a thin black leather shoulder belt passing under the scarlet sash.

Ranks
Officers
Colonel
Two laces of gold round and one of gold cord each of the sleeve cuffs
Lieutenant Colonel
Two laces of gold round each of the sleeve guns
Major
Like the previous one but only with a lace and a gold cord parallel to it.
Captain
Like the previous but without cord
Lieutenant
Two golden cords around each cannon
Ensign
A gold cord.
Note: Company officers have a yellow metal whistle attached to the uniform on the left side by means of a cord of the same metal.
Non-Commissioned Officers
Assistant Sergeant
Four black silk chevrons, placed on the right arm and stitched to the seams of the sleeve, with the apex facing the elbow side and a yellow metal crown in the centre of the last chevron that is to the side of the shoulder.

Quarter Master Sergeant
The same badges as the previous one but placed on the left arm.
First Sergeant
Four black silk chevrons on the right arm.
Second Sergeant
Three chevrons
Junior Sergeant
Same as above but left arm
Chief Trumpet
Same as the second sergeant.
Corporal
Two Chevrons of black wool on Right Arm
Lance Corporal
Chevron
Officers Slings
Black leather with yellow hardware
Note: The first and second sergeants had an ivory or bone whistle attached to the left side of the uniform by a black silk cord.

Cavalry

Up until the end of the Civil War, the Portuguese cavalry did not have a clear distinct tactical use. There were not heavy or light regiments, but one of the most renowned Miguelite cavalry units was the Chaves Cavalry Regiment, known also as the Chaves Dragoons. Only after the end of the Civil War and with the reorganization of the Portuguese Army was the cavalry finally divided into two lancer regiments and six *chasseurs à cheval* regiments. During the Civil War, the Miguelite Army relied mostly on the regular cavalry regiments, and some Royalist volunteer units raised in 1828: Monforte Cavalry Company of Royalist Volunteers, 1st and 2nd Cavalry companies of the Lisbon Royalist Volunteers. In 1834, and following the Liberal innovation of introducing lancers, the lancers company of the Royalist Volunteers of Salvaterra de Magos was formed in the Ribatejo province where the Miguelite Army was cornered by the advance of the Liberal Army towards the south. The creation of a lancer unit in the Miguelite Army was a considered attempt to obtain the same battlefield effective results as the Liberal lancers, created by Colonel Bacon during the Siege of Porto.

The Royalist Volunteers' cavalry uniforms are scarce in descriptions and sources, and very few engravings survive to the modern day. It is likely these units wore line cavalry uniforms, with blue short tailed coatees with different colour collars, cuffs, and piping. This was combined with white accoutrements, and leather reinforced blue, grey, or white trousers, along with high or ankle boots and box spurs. The head cover was probably the 1815 bell-topped shakos with scarlet plumes and a VR (Volunteers Royalists/Royalist Volunteers) brass plate at the front.

Armament was also of Army regulation, using older models like the 1796 English swords, both the straight and curved blade. The firearms, if available, were the Portuguese or English carbines and pistols from Peninsular War vintage, as already described for the cavalry line regiments. With regard to the

Salvaterra de Magos Lancers Company, there is no description of the unit except for a very rare coloured engraving showing two Miguelite lancers figures with dark blue coatees and grey trousers and Czapskas with red plumes. The lancer pennants show the Miguelite colours of red and blue.

The Liberal Army also had cavalry units formed outside the line regiments. In the Azores, a small cavalry corps known as the Guides Corps was raised. It was initially a 25 men squadron, later upgraded to 80 men, intended to perform reconnaissance and liaison duties more than full combat operations. After the beginning of the Siege of Porto, the English cavalry colonel, later brigadier general, Sir Anthony Bacon, raised and mustered a new cavalry regiment, the Queen's Lancers, with 80 Englishmen. Quickly the regiment consisted of 250 men and horses, and in 1834, on the Ribatejo front, the Queen's Lancers was a full 500 man cavalry unit including British, Portuguese, French, and Belgian troopers. From the first, the Queen's Lancers were dressed in British style, with scarlet short tailed coatees, blue collars and cuffs, white piping's, winter blue overalls or white for the summer, with black leather boots and box spurs. Their armament were the Portuguese standard issue with English or Portuguese flintlock pistols and the English 1821 cavalry sword, and, of course, the regulation bamboo lance with long irons, probably the 1820 model. The lance pennant was blue and white, the colours of the constitutional monarchy. The Queen's Lancers wore the traditional Czapskas in black leather with a brass trim at the visor. The squared top was in scarlet cloth with a long fallen red plume and the blue and white cocardes.

For the regular cavalry regiments between 1815 and 1834 the primary features were as it follows:

Cavalry Regiments facings 1815-34

1815 1834	Coat	Collar	Cuffs	Piping	Summer Trouser	Winter Trouser	Plumes	Accoutrements
nº 1	Blue	White	White	White	White	Blue	Scarlet	White
nº 2	Blue	White	White	Scarlet	White	Blue	Scarlet	White
nº3	Blue	White	White	Yellow	White	Blue	Scarlet	White
nº 4	Blue	Scarlet	Scarlet	White	White	Blue	Scarlet	White
nº 5	Blue	Scarlet	Scarlet	Scarlet	White	Blue	Scarlet	White
nº 6	Blue	Scarlet	Scarlet	Yellow	White	Blue	Scarlet	White
nº 7	Blue	Yellow	Yellow	White	White	Blue	Scarlet	White
nº 8	Blue	Yellow	Yellow	Scarlet	White	Blue	Scarlet	White
nº 9	Blue	Yellow	Yellow	Yellow	White	Blue	Scarlet	White
nº 10	Blue	Light Blue	Light Blue	White	White	Blue	Scarlet	White
nº 11	Blue	Light Blue	Light Blue	Scarlet	White	Blue	Scarlet	White
nº 12	Blue	Light Blue	Light Blue	Yellow	White	Blue	Scarlet	White

Shako, Overalls and Boots

The Portuguese Cavalry adopted the English style bell-topped shako introduced in 1811. Later designated the 1815 model, it remained in service until the Uniform Plan of 1834. Made of hard leather with a tin flap except the top and the flap, which was varnished. They would have an iron rim inside the top and a brass reinforcement on the top to add protection against blows and down slashes from enemy swords. The plates were the same as the 1810 model until 1832 when Liberal troops adopted the new shako plates of Queen Dona Maria II. They wore a lace of gold around the top. The officers could use velveteen or velvet to cover the shako. The chin strap would be brass chain. The overalls or trousers would be in the regulation blue for the winter or white for summer, always with an inner leg leather reinforcement to prevent friction against the saddle. The boots were of two models and always in hardened black leather. The first was the 1806/1810 model knee-length boots to wear over the riding pants with box spurs. A later model, from 1811 onwards, was also black leather, but in a shorter version, ankle boots, to wear beneath new reinforced overalls introduced in 1811, again with box spurs.

Coats

Officers and NCO'S

Manufactured from Prussian blue cloth with short tails in all ranks, the high collar and sleeve cuffs had the distinctive regimental colours. The officers had golden fringed metal epaulettes and the NCOs had similar epaulettes, but the fringes were of silk cord, and from 1815 the sergeant's ranks were of the British style with yellow silk chevrons according to each graduation.

Ranks

Same as the officers and NCO with the regimental distinctive colours.

Swords and Firearms

In the Peninsular War, the Portuguese cavalry still sparsely employed the old Model 1806 cavalry sword with curved blade, brass furniture, and iron scabbard. Throughout that same period the British reorganization provided the Portuguese Cavalry with the 1796 heavy cavalry sword as well the 1796 light cavalry sabre with steel and iron furniture and scabbards. Issued in thousands, the 1796 heavy sword was in service with the Cavalry City Guards until 1851. These swords were in broad use during the Miguelite Wars. Also employed was the English 1821 sword which was later copied by the Army Royal Arsenal as regulation issue in the 1834 uniform plan.

The firearms of the Portuguese Cavalry were the flintlock smoothbore carbines, mostly of English import, namely the Paget Model and the 1796 carbine of .65. bore, both with slings. It is known that the pistols were mainly the English New Land and Dragoon models, but also Portuguese copies from the Royal Arsenals and civil contractors. This is because of firearm copies manufactured in Porto and Braga, between 1816-17, which are on display atthe Porto Military Museum. These swivel ramrods pistols of .65 and .75 bore, were kept in pairs in saddle holsters. There is no full description of the lance but it was probably the 1816 or 1820 English pattern or even the 1823 French model. Having a blue and white pennant just above the spearhead, these were also copied by Porto arsenals or civilian blacksmiths, having a blue and white pennant just above the spearhead.

Pouch Belt and Carbine slide

In white leather and yellow brass hardware. Yellow metal plate with embossed Royal Arms in silver. Later models of the Liberal example had the Queen Dona Maria II Royal Arms. Normally the pouch was made of black leather with brass edgings and regimental ornaments normally fit for 20 or 30 pistol cartridges or carbine ammunition.

Sabretache

Made in black leather with royal arms, suspended under sword scabbard.

Saddles

From the Peninsular War period, the saddles were of English or a very similar Portuguese model with small trunks, the rear seat wider and higher than the opposite side. This was placed on a blue backdrop blanket with regimental colour linings, which covered the horse from shoulders to hips.

Shabraque and Holsters

The saddle was covered by a Prussian blue shabraque trimmed all around by regimental colour. It covered the saddle and the horse from shoulder to hip over the issue cloth blanket. Leather holsters were covered with chaplets of Prussian blue cloth and both, as with the shabrackes, are garnished with lace or embroidered and gilded lace according to the patent of its wearer.

Ranks
Officers
Colonel
Two laces of gold round and one of gold cord each of the sleeve cuffs
Lieutenant Colonel
Two laces of gold round each of the sleeve cuffs.
Major
Like the previous one but only with a lace and a gold cord parallel to it.
Captain
Like the previous but without cord
Lieutenant
Two gold cords around each cuff
Ensign
A gold cord
Note: Company officers have a yellow metal whistle attached to the uniform on the left side by means of a chain of the same metal
Non-Commissioned Officers
Assistant Sergeant
Four golden lace chevrons, placed on the right arm and nailed to the seams of the sleeve, with the apex facing the elbow side and a yellow metal crown in the centre of the last chevron that is to the side of the shoulder.
Quarter Master Sergeant
The same badges as the previous one but placed on the left arm.

First Sergeant
Four golden lace chevrons on the right arm.
Second Sergeant
Three chevrons
Junior Sergeant
Same as above but left arm
Chief Trumpet
Same as the second sergeant.
Corporal
Two chevrons of yellow wool on right arm
Lance Corporal
One chevron of yellow wool on right arm

Artillery

In 1808, with the beginning of the English military support and the appointment of William Carr Beresford as Marshal Commander of the Portuguese Army, articulating with the Council of Regency, the organization of the logistics of war materials and weapons had a new impetus. This followed the parameters of the British models and standards. With the end of the second French Invasion in spring 1809, the full reorganization of the Portuguese Army also included the Artillery. Significant improvements to ordnance being made, the lighter yet sturdier English carriage was adopted and the 6-inch howitzers replaced by the 5.5-inch English ones. The 3, 6, 9 and 12-pounder field guns were continued, although the 3-pounder light gun was reclassified to the mountain artillery category in 1811.

The artillery ammunition was manufactured by the Royal Arsenals of Lisbon and Porto or imported from England during the Peninsular War. It had some innovative features such as the shrapnel shot, which was a fragmentation round. This ammunition, with devastating effects on infantry and cavalry, consisted of a hollow, thin-walled sphere with a load of metallic spheres and black powder inside. The fuse was made of wood; these fuses began to ignite after firing, and the bursting of the load was regulated by the size of the fuses, which could cause premature explosions. Another anti-personal device was the tin canister loaded with projectiles that could be of various calibres. The canister was terribly effective if fired at close range over large targets, including massive concentrations of infantry, advancing columns, or cavalry charges. Apart from this type of special ammunition, the most commonly used ordnance was the solid shot, the powder charged and fused bombs and grenades, the shrapnel cartridge, grape shot with the same objectives as the tin canister but with the cargo packed in a linen bag or canvas. Constant arsenal demands were determined by projectile numbers and required respective loads for each piece: 400 shots for a 9 lb field gun and 276 shots for a 6-field gun. A lighter 3-pounder gun was needed to consume 34,5 kg of gunpowder to fire 100 shots and 138 kg of iron to cast the solid shots; the 6-pounder gun also for 100 shots spent 68kg of gunpowder and 275 kg of iron for the solid shots and the 12-pounder field gun for 100 shots consumed 550 kg of gunpowder and 551 kg of iron for solid shot. From this we can determine the amount of gunpowder and cast iron that was needed to keep the Portuguese artillery efficient during operations, which was constituted until 1832 as follows:

1 5,5-inch howitzer
5 6-pounder field guns
78 ammunition vaults
1 campaign forge
94 howitzer cartridges (30 charges of 12 ounces of gunpowder and 64 of 16ounces)
650 6-pounder shots (450 solid shots and 200 canisters)
900 fuses
64 howitzer grenades
30 howitzer canisters

A brigade of this size mobilized 158 men, including officers, NCOs, and men and 117 mules, of which 54 were tracking mules and the remaining 63 were cargo mules. In addition to the ammunition, the brigade carried a substantial number of maintenance tools and reserves.

The artillery regiments, although largely dependent on arsenal logistics and the commissariat, had specialized personnel to perform field maintenance and repairs. There were also workers specializing in the manufacturing of ammunition and for regimental small arms. For this they had a so-called "laboratory", which in practice was a mobile workshop where all the materials and ingredients for the manufacturing of explosives such as gunpowder, saltpetre, sulphur, ordinary cartridge paper, wine spirit, pitch and tallow were found, as well as yellow wax, tar, turpentine, flaxseed oil, black and white pitch, ammonia and other products. There were four regiments in the country, which could deploy separate detachments of batteries. The regiments were also responsible, together with arsenals, for the operation and supervision of the fortresses artillery and its fixed garrisons.

Artillery Uniform facings 1815-34

1815 1834	Coat	Collar	Cuffs	Piping	Summer Trouser	Winter Trouser	Gaiters	Accoutrements
nº 1	Blue	Blue	Blue	Scarlet	White	Blue	Black	White
nº 2	Blue	Black	Black	Scarlet	White	Blue	Black	White
nº3	Blue	Black	Blue	Scarlet	White	Blue	Black	White
nº 4	Blue	Blue	Black	Scarlet	White	Blue	Black	White

Officers and NCOs

Bell-topped Shako

Like the Infantry, officer shakos were introduced in 1815. Made of leather with a tin flap, the top and the flap should be varnished and lined on the outside with black cloth. They would have had an iron rim inside the top and the plates were the same as the 1806/1810 models until 1832 when the Liberal troops adopted the new shako plates of Queen Dona Maria II. They wore a lace of gold around the top in cavalry style. The officers could also have velveteen or velvet covering the shako. The chin strap was of brass scales. This kind of shako was adopted by the new mounted artillery units in the late 1820's and in the Civil War.

Ranks

Stovepipe Shako
Of leather and thick card frame with a black leather flap and lined on the outside in black fabric. The plates were the same as those in the 1806/1810 model until 1832, when the Liberal troops adopted new shako plates. There were no chin straps, the shako's uprightness depending on a perfect fit onto the soldier's head.

All Ranks

Coat and trousers
From 1815-34, the Portuguese artillery wore the same pattern of uniforms as the Infantry. Their uniforms were also dark blue, similar in cut and design as well. From 1815 the shoulder wings were introduced, also in blue and scarlet fabric. The officers had golden fringed metal epaulettes. The NCOs from 1815 followed the British style, wearing yellow silk chevrons according to each graduation. The 1815 regulations for the trousers or pantaloons were the Prussian blue winter model, and for the summer, white linen or canvas, always covering the black cloth gaiters. The shoes were made of black leather. Later some artillery units were reclassified as mounted artillery batteries, and the uniforms were of cavalry pattern, with artillery plates.

Vest
Of blue wool cloth with sleeves, usually called police coats, similar to the British shell jackets.

Overcoat
Of grey blend thick woollen cloth.

Armament
During the Peninsular War the Portuguese line infantry was armed with English Brown Bess flintlock muskets, which were initially also to be the standard weapon for the foot artillery. However, later orders from the Portuguese War Office, due to the lack of enough muskets for the infantry and militia regiments, determined that the artillerymen were to be armed only with a pistol and a short sword, from 1809 and later years, until the Civil War. Artillery officers had the 1806 model infantry sword, which lasted until 1832, except for the Liberal Army, in which the artillery officers used several sword patterns of foreign purchase, mostly English and French models. The Liberal Army regular artillerymen used the short sword, but volunteer artillery units like the Academic Company (former University of Coimbra students) used flintlock infantry muskets and carbines of assorted origins. Only after 1834 and the end of the Civil War, was the Portuguese Artillery reorganized into foot and mounted regiments. They were then issued with standard Brown Bess muskets, until the late 1840's for the foot units, and English cavalry carbines for the horse artillery.

Artillery Ordnance (Plates 4, 5, 17 and 18)
The main field artillery for this period was:

3 pounder light gun
Manufactured in Portugal
Bore – 3 pounds (7,5 cm)
Campaign employment and troop support
Ammunition: canisters, grapeshot and 3 pounds solid shot (1,4 kg)
Range from 250 up to 1000 metres
Used from 1763 onwards, first in Portuguese manufactured Valleré carriages, replaced by English carriages from 1809 until the 1840s.

6 pounder field gun
Manufactured in England and Portugal
Bore – 6 pounds (9,9 cm)
Campaign employment and troop support
Ammunition: canisters, grapeshot and 6 pounds solid shot (2,8 kg)
Range from 275 up to 1280 metres
Used from 1804 onwards, first in Portuguese manufactured carriages, replaced by English carriages from 1809 until the 1840s

9 pounder field gun
Manufactured in England and Portugal
Bore – 9 pounds (10,9 cm)
Campaign employment and siege operations
Ammunition: canisters, grapeshot and 9 pounds solid shot (4 kg), including coastal defence chain shot
Range from 330 up to 2200 metres
Purchased during the Peninsular War with English carriages until the 1840s

12 pounder field gun
Manufactured in England and Portugal
Bore – 12 pounds (11,7 cm)
Campaign employment and siege operations
Ammunition: canisters, grapeshot and 12 pounds solid shot (4 kg), including coastal defence chain shot
Range from 645 up to 4300 metres
Purchased during the Peninsular War with English carriages until the 1840s

6 inches howitzer
Manufactured in Portugal
Bore – 6 inches (15,5 cm)
Campaign employment and siege operations
Ammunition: canisters, grapeshot and 3 pounds grenades or bombs (1,4 kg)
Range with ½ pound of gunpowder 180 up to 360 m; with 1 pound of gunpowder 400 up to 800 m
Used from 1774 onwards, first in Portuguese manufactured Valleré carriages, replaced by English carriages from 1809 until the 1840s.

5,5 inches howitzer
Manufactured in England and Portugal
Bore – 5,5 inches (15,2 cm)
Campaign employment and siege operations
Ammunition: canisters, grapeshot and 3 pounds grenades or bombs (1,4 kg)
Range with ½ pound of gunpowder 180 up to 360 m; with 1 pound of gunpowder 400 up to 800 m
Purchased during the Peninsular War with English carriages until the 1840s

12,5 inches howitzer
Manufactured in England and Portugal
Bore – 12,5 inches (31 cm)
Siege operations
Ammunition: canisters, grapeshot and 15 pounds grenade or bombs (6,8 kg)
Range with 8 pounds of gunpowder 1200 m; with 12 pounds of gunpowder 1400 m. With 8 pounds of gunpowder and 45º of elevation 2400 m; with 12 pounds of gunpowder and 15º of elevation 2800 m.
Purchased during the Peninsular War with English carriages until the 1840s

Aside from these models, there were also the mortars, most of them manufactured in the Royal Army arsenals in Lisbon, both from Portuguese and English models. With lesser mobility and fitted for siege operations, they were widely used during the Miguelite Wars, especially during the Siege of Porto. Most were of 6, 8, 12, 18 and 24 pounders, used mainly by the Miguelite siege artillery. The Liberal forces, soon after their landing near Porto, in July 1832, had only three or six (the sources do not agree on this subject) light field cannons which I believe to be 3 pounders. This small artillery force had been formed in the Azores, manned by the Academics Company, under the command of Captain Lieutenant José Maria Baldy. In 1831, a general staff and a battalion were formed of six companies for a total of 688 men commanded by the famous General Sebastião Drago Brito de Cabreira. This battalion was made up of four batteries, but as mentioned earlier, upon arrival at Porto, the Liberal army had only three (or six depending on the sources) light field guns, one of them at least from the time of D. Maria I (1797). These guns would soon be complemented by the fifty cannons and two howitzers that were on deposit at the Ouro Royal

Arsenal, probably from the 1809 campaigns, although the guns did not have any carriages. This forced the city carpenters and blacksmiths to build somewhat improvised carriages. The Miguelite General Santa Marta, former commander of the Porto garrison, in the retreat before D. Pedro's army, inexplicably did not destroy these guns. It was these assorted guns, since there is not any record of the models found in the arsenal, that formed the many batteries and the strongholds of the Porto defences between 1832-33. These were complemented by some naval guns landed from the lighter ships of the small Liberal navy. The hurriedly built fortifications protecting Porto and the nearer environs had the mission to face the batteries of the Miguelite Army that spread along the siege lines. From August 1832, and in the face of the deadlock between the Liberal and the Miguelite troops, the latter group far superior in numbers, it was decided to quickly fortify Porto to resist a longstanding siege. It was therefore necessary to lift these batteries into suitable locations to effectively cover the 12 km length of the Liberal lines.

Some facts, mixed with some 'myths', about the artillery of this time have come to light and persisted to this day. For example, the arrival and employment of the famous .Paixhans heavy howitzer cannon offered to D. Miguel by the rich and devoted merchant João Paulo Cordeiro. It was, in fact, a heavy naval gun of French manufacture, 22 cm bore, firing a 30kg shell, which meant that it had a long range and destructive power, mainly designed for siege fire and naval use. In fact, the *Paixhans* gun weighed 3,400 kg and the range of fire was just about over 3,500 m. it was said at the time that the *Paixhans* grenades fired from the Thunder battery (*bateria do Trovão*) managed to hit areas in Porto as distant as Santo Ovídio Square (present-day Republic Square) or the Santa Catarina and Cedofeita neighbourhoods in the northern outskirts of Porto. Regarding the large dimensions of the *Paixhans* gun, Joaquim Martins de Carvalho, in an article of the Conimbricense of 24 March 1832, stated he once saw it in transit through Condeixa, near Coimbra, in December 1832. It was hauled by thirteen oxen joints (up to twenty in some places) no doubt depending on the almost non-existent road network of the time.

The 15 January 1833 Constitutional Chronicle of Porto read as follows; on the *Paixhans* gun:

> In the absence of iron bullets, enemies are thrown at us with stone shots, bombs and clay grenades ... The latest are new foreign composition, the promised effect of which was the sighed fire of Porto. It is reported that the inventor of this instrument of ruin was promised great rewards by D. Miguel, and a rank of general in his army. But from experience, this rebel army learned today that the city is incombustible and its defenders invincible. What has not been doing a lot of bombing can hardly be stoned, still thrown by the catapult of João Paulo Cordeiro, - a new horse from whose broad bulge so long awaited the new enemies that would come out of the fires and the ruins of the new Troy! Bisarma, who saw in procession from Lisbon to Porto, beginning the killing and destruction that was expected of her by the joints of oxen that dragged her, and by the wheels, bolts and axles of the various cars that moved during the journey. (see Plate 19)

During the Siege of Porto came another weapon that was used was the Congrève type rocket launcher. Many authors of the time, such as Simão José da Luz Soriano in his book *History of the Siege of Porto*, refer to the use of this projectile during the civil war by Liberal troops. This gun was propelled by black gunpowder, and flight was stabilized by means of a stick or by ejection of gases through slanted holes in the rear, giving it a rotating motion and better shooting accuracy. The warheads could be solid shot or explosive shells, having above all a psychological effect on the enemy.

It was these types of guns that equipped the Liberal and Miguelite armies, forming batteries and strongholds of besieged and besiegers respectively. From the existing charts and documents, I found that the Miguelite batteries made heavy use of mortars, which is logical given that they were deployed to reach fortified targets, both civil and military. Moreover, the Miguelites had in their possession the aforementioned

Paixhans gun. Liberals mostly used field guns (due to the low number of available mortars) since the Ouro Royal Arsenal only mentions two 16-inch mortars, and in some recollections there are references to the use of heavy 24 pounder guns in the Liberal stronghold of the Serra of Pilar. The predominance of the field guns was nonetheless useful, as Porto's defence lines were often stormed by infantry and cavalry attacks, such as the battle of the 29 September 1832 and 25 July 1833, as well as in Vila Nova de Gaia, the assaults of 14 October, 8 November 1832 or 4 March 1833.

Ranks
Officers
Colonel
Two gold laces of gold one of gold cord each of the sleeve cuffs
Lieutenant Colonel
Two laces of gold on the sleeve cuffs
Major
Like the previous one but with a lace and a gold cord parallel to it.
Captain
Like the previous but without cord
Lieutenant
Two golden cords around each cannon
Ensign
A gold cord.
Note: Company officers have a yellow metal whistle attached to the uniform on the left side by means of a cord of the same metal.
Non-Commissioned Officers
Assistant Sergeant
Four gold lace chevrons, placed on the right arm and nailed to the seams of the sleeve, with the apex facing the elbow side and a yellow metal crown in the centre of the last chevron that is to the side of the shoulder.
Quarter Master Sergeant
The same badges as the previous one but placed on the left arm.
First Sergeant
Four golden lace chevrons on the right arm.
Second Sergeant
Three chevrons
Junior Sergeant
Same as above but left arm
Chief Trumpet
Same as the second sergeant.

Corporal
Two chevrons of yellow wool on right arm
Lance Corporal
A single chevron of yellow wool on right arm

Royal Engineers Corps

The Portuguese Engineering and Sappers Corps was born in 1647 with the creation, by decree of King D. João IV of Portugal, of the Sapper Worker Corps, which in 1793 gave place to the Royal Corps of Engineers of the Portuguese Army. This corps, at first composed of only engineer officers, had the task of directing the construction, defence and maintenance plans of fortifications, the construction and conservation of other military buildings and roads, the recognition of borders and regions, the lifting of maps, geographical and cartographic patterns and the layout of plans, topographic maps and military reports. Until 1812, the Corps of Engineers employed as labour force troops of other services, especially sappers and pontoniers integrated hitherto in the artillery regiments. That year, an engineering unit, the Engineer Battalion of Artificers, was founded, composed of troops of artisans, miners, sappers and pontoniers. This organization, up until the Miguelite Wars, was organized into regimental size. Engineer officers worked frequently with their artillery comrades, and most of their academic element shared common subjects. During the Miguelite Wars, the engineer officers, as well the sappers and artificers did an excellent job erecting fine fortification works both as the besieged and as besiegers, especially during the Siege of Porto. Their uniforms were basically the same in both armies. All ranks were already wearing the bell-topped shakos, the Royal Arms of D. Miguel in one part and on the other, those corresponding to Queen Dona Maria II. The coat was the infantry standard short tailed model in Prussian blue, black collars and cuffs (officer coats had velvet collars and cuffs), with white piping. The accoutrements were the white leather Infantry pattern, as well as being armed with the India Pattern flintlock musket. Other equipment consisted of issue shovels, picks, axes, saws, and engineering materials.

Liberal Army

Liberal Line Units 1828-34 (Plates 1 to 6)

D. Pedro needed reliable troops – his best Portuguese troops needed to be hardened, the others could not necessarily be relied upon. He therefore set out to raise foreign mercenaries. Here he had the invaluable help of the Spaniard Mendizábel, a financier and banker of Jewish extraction, tall and dark, a devout Liberal, determined to stop the slide into medieval barbarity in the Peninsula. He was able to raise the money to equip and arm a small fleet, manned mostly by British sailors – admittedly the sweepings of every port on the Southern coast – under the command of a British half-pay captain, George Rose Sartorius, with a small number of ex-Royal Navy officers to command the ships. Sartorius did not know what he was getting himself into. His crews were a drunken rabble, pay was rarely forthcoming, the ships were tired, the largest being 3 ex-East Indiamen that had seen better days and ended up being converted into frigates. It is quite impressive that he was able to create a credible navy at all, let alone one which held together for months on end in foul weather, in the face of constant near mutiny.

Soldiers were more of a problem. Pedro was helped by the July Revolution that unseated Charles X in France, in 1830, and the same year saw the fall of Wellington's government in Britain. While recruiting in France was relatively easy, the British Government was unwilling to sanction it, and the Foreign Enlistment

Act made any open recruiting without government approval impossible. Despite Miguelite spies and official dissatisfaction, recruiting was undertaken – for 'settlers in the Brazils' – although it proved difficult to get off the ground at first. Sir John Milley Doyle, a strange fantasist, was the first to become involved, promising much and delivering nothing, but once the hard-headed George Lloyd Hodges was engaged, things moved much faster. Hodges had served on the Peninsular and at Waterloo, was a confirmed Liberal, a strict disciplinarian and superb organizer. He contacted a core of reliable and efficient officers who began to recruit men in secret. It proved very hard - only 400 were raised, falling short of Pedro's expectations (he had hoped for 600 and even a figure of 1,200 men was drawn at one point). Pedro was not pleased with the men when they first landed on Terceira. Indeed, the police reckoned the crime rate in the St Giles district had almost disappeared once the recruits had gone, but Hodges soon licked them into shape. He had picked some excellent officers – notably Charles Shaw, a tall red-headed Scot who was first on the Pampelido beach, idealist, Puritan, utterly without fear, yet a mass of self-doubt. He too had served in the British Army.

The recruiting operations continued, becoming more open as events unfolded and public sympathy with the Liberal cause grew. Reinforcements dribbled in at first but by November 1832 with the siege in full swing, large numbers of British and other nationalities were arriving in Porto when the ships could get them in.

With regard to Portuguese troops, D. Pedro's Liberal Army had as its core, the 5th Caçadores Battalion which, in addition to the 18th Infantry Regiment, the Queen's Own Volunteers and the Academics Battalion, revolted on Terceira Island, Azores, in 1828, . Most emigrated to England, France, and Belgium after the failed Liberal coup that same year. These units formed the prime units of the Liberal Army in the Azores after the landings on Terceira Island in 1829-30. The Azores Liberal government legislation extinguished the old Militia and Ordenanças system and the Royalist Volunteers, though only in Liberal-controlled territories, and replaced them with fixed and mobile volunteer battalions, which were being formed as the Liberals conquered territory (the former appeared in Porto, then in the Algarve and Lisbon.). The desertions of Miguelite troops integrated the Liberal forces and allowed for their growth until they became an 8,300 men army ready to sail to mainland Portugal. The Liberal army was composed, upon landing at Pampelido, as follows:

- 2nd, 3rd, 5th and 12th Caçadores battalions.
- Queen's Own Volunteers organized as a light infantry unit.
- The Academic volunteers (initially used in the Azores as light infantry but later converted to mountain artillery battery commanders and also introducing the use of Congreve rockets).
- The Sacred Battalion (made up of officers, later deployed as commanders of the Porto Volunteer Battalions).
- The Guides Cavalry Squadron (soldiers and cavalry officers).
- Provisional 18th Infantry Regiment as Provisional (with 1 battalion of the 3rd Infantry Regiment, 1 battalion of the 6th Infantry Regiment and 1 battalion of the 10th Infantry Regiment and a few squads of the 15th Regiment, plus circa 200 Azorean men to replenish mainly the 18th Infantry Regiment).
- National Artillery Regiment.
- Navy Regiment (made up of English troops).
- Portuguese *Tiralleurs* Battalion (French and Belgian troops).

Following the landing between Mindelo and Pampelido and the occupation of Porto, the Liberal Army gradually reorganized some of the original units. Thereafter, the Sacred Battalion, the Guides and the Provisional 18th Regiment disappeared. As referred earlier the Sacred Battalion was disbanded and all the officers were detached to command the increasing Porto Volunteer Battalions. The Guides squadron was attached to the Liberal headquarters and also detached for other cavalry units, and the Provisional 18th Infantry Regiment quickly become the 18th Infantry Regiment, the 6th Infantry Regiment and the 10th Infantry Regiment.

Other regiments and battalions were raised or reformed:

- 10th and 11th Cavalry Regiments.
- Queen's Lancers raised by Colonel Anthony Bacon (by the end of the war there were 2 lancer regiments which would be the core of this corps after the 1834 reorganization).
- Fixed and mobile Volunteers Battalions (mainly from Porto and Lisbon, often commanded by the regular Army officers).

Foreign military units serving with the Liberal Army, were divided by the following regiments or corps:

1. The French, Belgians, Germans, Italians and other nationalities were organized as follows:

- Battalion of Portuguese *Tiralleurs* that would divide into:
- 1st Regiment of Light Infantry of the Queen,
- 2nd Regiment of Light Infantry of the Queen, which includes an Italian company.
- Ramorino French Volunteer Regiment.

2. English, Irish and Scottish units were as follows:

Navy Regiment divided into:

- 1st Regiment of the Navy Brigade,
- 2nd Regiment of the Navy Brigade.
- Regiment of Queen's Own Grenadiers or Irish Grenadiers.
- Scottish Marines Regiment.
- Royal British Grenadier Regiment.

3. The Belgian forces included:

- Queen's 2nd Light Infantry Regiment.
- Portuguese *Tiralleur* Corps, later the Belgian or Le Charlier *Tiralleur* Corps. The corps consisted of 8 infantry companies, including one of grenadiers and one of artillery, with Coehorn mortars and possibly a small squad of 30 lancers.

4. The Spanish, deployed in 1834, under the effective command of General Rodil:

Battalion of Spanish Light Infantry of the Guadiana.

Liberal Army Uniforms

Liberal uniforms were the most altered, but overall retained most of the characteristics of the 1815 regulations. Liberal officers wore a similar uniform to that worn in the Miguelite Army. This was unlike the American Civil War 30 years later during which Union and Confederate troops had their own issue uniforms, but not necessarily blue or grey. The 5th Caçadores Battalion and the 18th Infantry Regiment appear to have been able to maintain the same uniform as the 1815 regulations. The remaining regiments and battalions, which had to be rebuilt, adopted a simplified uniform:

> When available, the shakos were in the bell-topped model with a diamond-like plate and scale chin straps, but the old stove pipe model was likely still in use. The Caçadores or Light Infantry kept the same kind of shako worn in the Peninsular War period.

The majority of the coats had no back flaps (shell jackets) or were short tailed with peaked cuffs, mainly blue for all regular units, except those of the Caçadores, which were brown. The distinctive colours were the same of the Peninsular War.

Line artillery gunners also wore the regulation blue uniforms and shakos, but the volunteer artillerymen, most of them in Porto or Lisbon, adopted the simpler uniform with forage caps, blue or grey shell jackets, and trousers of the same colour. The same happened with the Liberal line cavalry, though the newly raised Bacon's Lancers have a short tailed red uniform and a Czapska cap with a skull and bones plate bearing the motto "Death or Glory". There is no consensus across sources with regard to the Guides cavalry corps. Indeed, in illustrations of the period a soldier is depicted in a blue shell jacket, grey trousers and blue peakless cap, whilst in the narrative history of the Siege of Porto by Luz Soriano, refers to this unit clad in red jackets. Morever, illustrations in Soriano's book and others depict a Guides cavalryman with the blue jacket.

Porto City Volunteers wore different shades of blue, grey, or brown uniforms (cheaper cloth or whatever was available in a besieged city) in the same style as line regiment barracks uniforms, but favoured the use of forage caps, with or without peaks. The Academics Battalion, also known as company or corps, began wearing long tailed blue uniforms with a white breastplate, collars, and white cuffs (bought in France) probably with red trousers. Later, in the Azores, they began to wear short jackets in black or a very dark brown colour wool with black collars and cuffs, bright red piping and peaked forage cap, also in black or brown. The Queen's Own Volunteers wore the same kind of jackets, in Caçadores brown, but with a white collar and light blue cuffs.

Foreign units wore their national uniforms or special uniforms, normally with the blue and white cockades on shakos as well as the Royal Arms of Dona Maria II shako plates. The uniforms of the Navy Regiment (an all English unit) were the typical redcoat with a white piping, blue collars and cuffs. All other foreigners wore French style long tailed coats with red collars and cuffs.All other foreigners wore French style long tailed coats with red collars and cuffs. From the beginning of 1834, the Scottish Marines began to wear red jackets with pointed cuffs and white collar. The Belgians of the 2nd Light Infantry Regiment were distinguished by yellow leather belts and their Italian company wore green jackets and shakos and forage caps, with red cuffs and collars and, perhaps, bright white piping. Le Charlier's Belgian light infantry companies initially wore blue frock coats, but these were replaced by brown examples. The typical Belgian round feathered cap was also worn. It was fashionable among Liberals to have long beards: these were sported by Portuguese soldiers as a promise to Princess Dona Maria da Glória, daughter of D. Pedro. Their facial hair would remain uncut until she became Queen of Portugal, the 18th Infantry Regiment exclusive to this practice.

In general, the organization and structure of both armies remained the same following the English reorganization during the Peninsular War. The same applies to uniforms, although the influence of French and, above all, British and Prussian military influence is oversimplified. This was especially true with regard to barrack uniforms worn in combat ones. These were much akin the British uniforms worn during 1830s colonial campaigns and the First Afghan War (1839-42) and the simple and sober Landwehr uniforms of the various Prussian states. Tactics and combat doctrine remained the same as that employed during the Napoleonic period: the infantry defence square against cavalry attacks; infantry defence line and fire by ranks; attack column, or employment of light infantry and rifleman units. Siege warfare also followed Peninsular War doctrine, using heavily fortified lines with palisades, pits, earth walls connecting small forts and enclosed artillery batteries garrisoned with guns and mortars of assorted calibres on the Liberal side. The Miguelite Army also used siege lines organized in the same way, but with a much more standard siege artillery park, using heavy guns, howitzers and mortars up to the 36 pounder siege guns.

The evolution of the Liberal Army from the 8 July 1832 landing to May 1833 is depicted in the list below. It is based on one published by William Bollaert who was serving with the Gentleman Rifle Cadets during the siege of Porto:

Liberal Army from July 1832 to May 1833 (Bollaert) (see Plates 1 to 6)	**Ranks**
Portuguese Line Regiments	
6th Line Infantry	600
10th Line Infantry	600
18th Line Infantry	500
Portuguese Light Infantry (Caçadores)	
2nd Battalion	400
3rd Battalion	400
5th Battalion	400
Foreign Units and Volunteer Battalions (see Plates 7 to 9)	
1st Queen's Own Regiment (Portuguese, French and Belgians, the latter forming the Portuguese Tirailleurs Battalion)	1950
2nd Queen's Own Regiment (Germans, Poles, Italians)	650
1st English Battalion (former Navy Battalion)	200
2nd English Battalion	300
Scottish Battalion and Gentleman Rifle Cadets	140
Bacon's Lancers Regiment	200
Irish Battalion	330
Dodgin's Regiment	300
Artillery Corps (Portuguese and foreign troops)	1000
Academic Corps (Portuguese)	150
Officers Cavalry Corps	80

National and Porto Volunteers see Plates 10 to 13	
Movable Battalions	400
City Volunteer Battalions	5000
Total of Liberal Army in Porto May 1833	**14,300**

According to a Report from the Liberal War Cabinet regarding the period from 1828-34, we can see the evolution of the Liberal Army from the 8 July 1832, the day they landed in Portugal until 1 June 1834, as follows:

8 July 1832: Landing between Arnosa de Pampelido and Mindelo beaches. Portuguese sources mention 7,500 men; however, English recollections refer to 8,300 men. There is no clear reason for such a discrepancy, unless the foreign sources were already counting with the Belgians who arrived a few months later.	1 Battalion of Officers (the Sacred Battalion)
	1 Académicos (Academics) Company (sometimes also referred as Battalion)
	6 Line Infantry Battalions comprising 3 Regiments – the 6th, the 10th and the 18th
	3 Light Infantry Battalions (Caçadores) – the 2nd, the 3rd and the 5th.
	1 National Artillery Battalion
	The Queens Own Volunteers Battalion (later a Regiment)
	The Navy Battalion (English and Scots)
	The Portuguese *Tirailleurs* (French and Germans)
Siege of Porto	
1 January 1833	12,668 men, including the first 1,100 Belgians, the Italians and the massive City Volunteer Battalions
1 March 1833	18,340 men, with the increase of the Volunteer Battalions and Line units forces and the arrival of more foreign troops.
Southern Front	
1 September 1833 (Lisbon and Santarém)	36,429 men, the majority of which were in the Lisbon lines after Duke da Terceira's occupation of the Portuguese capital in the 24th of July 1833.
1 January 1834 (Ribatejo province operations front)	50,596 men, including many former Miguelite units that were transferred to the Queens service, as well as the Volunteer units from Lisbon.
1 June 1834 (Ribatejo and Alentejo operations front)	60,119 men, many former Miguelite units that were transferred to the Queens service, as well as the Volunteer units from Lisbon, comprising: 6 Cavalry Regiments, including the new Lancers Regiment, 17 Line Infantry Regiments, 5 Caçadores Battalions, 3 Artillery Regiments, 1 Academics Company, 1 Engineers Corps, 1 Artificers and Sappers Battalion and 1 Telegraphic unit (Signal Corps)

Foreigners in the Liberal Army (Plates 7 to 9)

The foreign volunteer troops were a very important part of the Liberal Army since their formation in Belle Isle, France, before leaving to the Azores and then to continental Portugal. Many wore uniforms brought from their own countries, only changing the rosette of their shakos or caps, (ex. Belgians of Le Charlier and British troops of the Navy Battalion). The Belgians contributed over 2,000 men. D. Pedro and his staff were looking for troops to raise a credible army. Like the British and the French, the Belgians took the opportunity to offer him the services of some undesirable veterans of Belgian struggle for independence. The first Belgian battalion was discharged on 8 September 1832 and transferred to the Liberal Army in Porto. In October 1832 it landed under fire of Miguelite artillery. A second battalion was recruited from penal companies and convicts of Aalst military prison. In Portuguese service, this second unit was known as, not without irony, 'the Walloon Guards (*Waalse Gardes*).' From the close of 1832 to early 1833, Belgium sent 1,100 men to Portugal. D. Pedro recruited two more Belgian battalions in late 1833. Between October 1833 and April 1834, another 1,100 men were sent to Portugal. Of those, the second battalion, called the Riflemen of Portugal (Batalhão de Atiradores Portugueses, later Batalhão de Atiradores Belgas), was raised by its commander, Major Le Charlier. Le Charlier had been the commander of the Riflemen of the Meuse (*Tirailleurs de Maas*) and was, in 1832, the commander of the Bruges Civil Guard. The Belgian uniform was similar in style to that of the Volunteers of Capiaumont (*Partizanen van Capiaumont*), but in blue overcoats with red piping, brown trousers and black top hats with green feathers. Officers had golden epaulettes and red piping in the collar and cuffs, red sash and a sword of unknown model. The other ranks are described as having red collars and cuffs, red cloth epaulettes and white accoutrements, later changed to black, as they had companies of light infantry (*De Belgische Militaire Expeditie te Portugal*). There were 1,100 men more divided between the two units. They shared 8 companies, including a grenadier company and an artillery company, the latter equipped with Belgian Coehorn mortars. Their standard weapon was the Liège flintlock musket and bayonet. The Queen presented the Belgian Corps with their standard on the 23 January 1834.

Amongst those who served in Portugal, most of the foreign units wore uniforms in the colours of their country such as the English, Scottish and Irish, with their famous redcoats and the French in the traditional blue coats, although it is unclear if they brought the new red trousers or remained with the white ones of the old model. Others were equipped with export material, like the small Italian corps of 90 men wearing French style uniforms, with bell-topped shakos and forage caps, probably the new French style red trousers or summer white versions, and distinctive green coats, instead of the French blue. The Italians, under French command, were issued with Baker Rifles and black accoutrements. Despite there being no clear explanation for this, it is believed that the Italians came from Genova and Milan and belonged to the freedom movements from Mazzini and young Garibaldi. They had escaped Austrian persecution and most were former Cacciatori and Carabiniere Genovese troops, well drilled in the use of rifles. Some units are almost unknown in Portuguese historical sources like the Gentleman Rifle Cadets, where William Bollaert was an officer. He described a small unit initially composed of 40 men:

> On the 10th our party, some forty in number, of gentlemen volunteers—now denominated Dom Pedro's Rifles, being considered as cadets—were ordered to the parade ground of the Seminario,

> the barracks of the greater number of the English. Dom Pedro came with Sir J.M. Doyle, making a long and thoughtful visit for inspection.[2]

According to this, the Gentleman Volunteers or Gentleman Rifle Cadets, wore green jackets and trousers, with black collars and cuffs, and black piping. In his writings, no mention is made of headgear (would a shako have been worn or a forage cap instead?). However, he is quite clear on the use of the Baker rifles issued to them, which implies that the accoutrements were in black leather and the ones suited for the use of the Baker rifles. This unit was attached to the Scottish troops under the command of Major Robert Shaw. The Rifle Cadets were outfitted in the British Rifle Brigade pattern adopted from the older 95th Rifles and the Kings German Legion from the Peninsular War era. The British troops are described in almost every English source as dressing in red or scarlet, as referred to in Knight, Doyle, Napier, Hodges and other recollections and memoires of British officers serving in the Liberal Army. If following British patterns, the trousers would have been grey or white depending on the weather; there is no clear mention of shakos yet the peakless forage caps would have surely been present. The Scottish units also followed this trend of bringing their own regulation uniforms, despite being in foreign service. The sources refer to the Scottish soldiers as former 71st and 52nd regiments rank and file, wearing the red coatees with regimental tartan trousers and peaked forage caps in black cloth with a band of tartan wool with feathers. Many of these men were already Peninsular War veterans and knew Portuguese territory quite well.

Liberal Army: National Volunteer Battalions (Plates 10 to 13)

The period concerning the War of the Two Brothers is prolific in the creation of volunteer units in both armies, Miguelite and Liberal. Many of these corps were raised as battalions, brigades, or companies, and rarely as regiments. According to sources and studies it was uncommon for a volunteer battalion to have the full number of required men. If a battalion was supposed to have 600-700 men, it was frequent for there to only end up being from 180 to 300 soldiers. This was a reality in both armies. It is indeed difficult to get a precise description of the uniforms of volunteers, but there is official documentation describing them as, for example, the 1828-32 Army Orders of the Day, more precisely from the 19 July 1832 (already issued in Porto) in which the decrees are issued. The National Battalions uniforms follow those of the Queen's Own Volunteers Battalion, which were of simple design. We do not know to what extent the order was fully complied with, but what may be a settled point is that these uniforms were nothing more than models based on the barrack and duty uniforms, commonly the jacket (English shell jacket), the trousers (already with central placket and no hatch) and boots or ankle boots. To this, a forage cap, with or without peak, was added; they were easier to produce and cheaper than a shako. The accoutrements were normally a leather belt, in black or leather in its natural colour with bayonet frog. In the same colours there was a cross belt holding the ammunition pouch. Due to the financial difficulties and logistics, the Liberal National Volunteer battalions were equipped and clothed in this pattern and the uniform colours varied between different shades of blue, brown, or grey, depending on the availability of the suppliers. In various sources such as the Porto City Hall ledgers, blue, brown, and grey fabrics are mentioned, matching the engravings in Luz Soriano's civil war history. These fabrics, a kind of "slop" clothing, came from abroad and were disembarked at Foz and carried by footmen, along with many other things, through the dangerous Ouro road boarding the Douro River up to the city of Porto, in

2 William Bollaert, *Wars of Succession of Portugal, and Spain from 1826 to 1840 with resume of the political History of Portugal and Spain to the presente time.* (London: Charing Cross, 1870). Vol. I, p. 102.

the night and under the fire of the Miguelite artillery batteries on the southern bank of the Douro river. The Constitutional Chronicle of Porto mentioned the need for the wives of the volunteers to go to police stations to lift the fabric cubits needed to make their husbands' uniforms and having to see the uniform models in printed posters.

It is noteworthy that it is possible that most of D. Pedro's foreign troops brought their original uniforms, because in archaeological excavations at the Miguelite Fort of Ervilha (Lordelo heights) English buttons were found, but with the Prince of Wales feathers on the back, which would exclude that it was an export button. In addition, the button was on the outer perimeter, which would indicate that it had fallen in one of the attacks of the English battalions under the command of Colonel Charles Shaw.

From 16 May 1828 onwards, 28 battalions of 'D. Pedro Volunteers' were created, which lasted until the Siege of Porto. One the most famous was the Queen's Own Volunteers Battalion, known for their long beards and for wearing brown shell jackets with white collars with bright blue piping, and light blue cuffs with bright white piping, then a brown forage cap with a light blue strip band. The accoutrements were black. The battalion's equipment set the standard for the volunteer battalions raised in the City of Porto during the siege of 1832-33, and in Lisbon, for its simplicity and easiness to produce. This was instead of the expensive and difficult tailoring of line regiment models, a trend certainly followed by line units due to the natural uniforms wear without proper supply replenishment.

The Academics Corps (or battalion, though some sources also refer to this unit as a company), initially raised in the Peninsular War and reformed during the Liberal exile in France, began wearing long tailed blue coats with white plastron, collar, and white cuffs, probably with scarlet trousers in the new French style (1830 regulations) of recent manufacture. They also wore a bell-topped shako, but this made for an expensive uniform that was somewhat contested within the ranks of that unit, old Coimbra University students, used to wearing their traditional black clothes. Still in 1831, in the Azores Islands, they would have received the light infantry shortened muskets instead of rifles. The Academics, after the landing in Portugal, were detached as artillerymen due to their status as former university students and most of them were distributed amongst the artillery of besieged Porto. Whilst there, they began to wear black or brown short jackets, brown collars and black cuffs with scarlet piping and a matching forage cap.

The July 1832 legislations provided for the use of shako and some engravings show it to be similar to that of Caçadores, but it was impossible to have the money and resources to dress the volunteers as line soldiers or even the full uniform of the light infantry. As stated above, it was the Queens Own Battalion who set the standard for uniforms for the hundreds of Porto volunteers that formed the mobile and fixed battalions. In contravention of the expensive July 1832 regulations forage caps, with and without peaks, were quickly adopted. It was easier to provide simple and cheap forage caps in a sieged city than the flashy light infantry shakos. The distinction of the various battalions was made by the colour of the cuffs and collars. Metal clips or emblems would be worn on the collars and on the front of the forage caps. It is not known how the ranks were identified, if by chevrons or laces in the cuffs. For these battalions, the officer ranks uniforms were quite similar to those of other ranks, including the forage caps yet excluding the wide use of long frockcoats with waist scarlet sashes and the sword belt.

Another celebrated unit, short-lived though it was, was an all officers Sacred Battalion. They were dressed in long tailed scarlet coats with blue collar, cuffs and perhaps, blue plastrons and white piping. Their own ranks were distinguished by the band, laces or epaulettes and sword. Later on, during the Siege of Porto, this unit was disbanded in order to detach these officers as commanders of the Porto volunteer battalions.

As for the Lisbon Volunteers, some dressed in the old uniforms of the Lisbon units, disbanded by express orders from D. Miguel (Trade Volunteers, Malta Corps, etc.). In late 1833 and early 1834, some militia regiments defected entirely to the Liberal Army and could retain their uniform and battle flag, changing only the Royal Arms to the Queen's colours. During the Miguelite Wars, many corps, regiments or battalions made up of civilian volunteers often continued to dress in civilian attire, carrying military accoutrements and weaponry. They should not be confused with numerous guerrilla parties that popped up everywhere and from both sides.

Liberal Army: Volunteer National Battalion facings 1832-34
See Plates 10 to 13

1832-34	Coat	Trousers	Collar	Cuffs	Piping	Forage Caps	Accoutrements
Academics Battalion	Brown	Brown	Black	Black	Red	Brown with red piping	Black
Cavalry Company (Guides)	Blue	Grey	Light Blue	Light Blue	White	Peakless cap Blue with light blue piping	White
Queen's Own Volunteer Battalion (later expanded to two Regiments in 1834)	Brown	Brown	White	Blue	Black	Brown with blue band	Black
1st Mobile Battalion	Brown	Brown	Blue	Brown	Black	Brown with blue band	Black
2nd Mobile Battalion	Grey	Grey	Grey	Blue	Black	Grey with blue band	Black
3rd Mobile Battalion (defenders of the Serra of Pilar Convent, a.k.a. Polacos da Serra)	Grey Blue	Grey Blue	Medium blue	Medium Blue	Black	Peakless cap Grey blue with blue medium blue band and tuft	Black
1st Fix/Garrison Battalion	Brown	Brown	Brown	Brown	Black	Blue with light band and white piping	Natural leather
2nd Fix/Garrison Battalion	Brown	Brown	White	Red	Black	Brown with red band	Natural leather
1st Provisional Battalion of Santa Catarina	Grey	Grey	Blue	White	Black	Grey	Natural leather

2nd Provisional Battalion of Santo Ovidio	Grey	Grey	Grey	Grey	Black	Grey	Black
3rd Provisional Battalion of Cedofeita	Grey	Grey	Blue	Grey	Black	Grey with grey tuft	Black
Craftsman Company of the 1st Fix/Garrison Battalion	Grey	Grey	Blue	Red	Black	Grey	White
Lampion Keepers Company	Grey	Grey	Light grey	Grey	Black	Grey	Black
Public Employees Battalion	Grey	Grey	Grey	Grey	Black	Grey with black tuft	Black
Beira Baixa (province) Battalion	Grey	Grey	Blue	Blue	Black	Grey with blue band	Black
Beira Alta (province) Battalion	Brown	Brown	Yellow	Grey	Black	Brown with yellow and black piping	Black
Trás-os-Montes (province) Battalion	Grey	Grey	Red	Medium Blue	Black	Grey with red piping	Black
Minho (province) Battalion	Grey	Grey	Green	Green	Black	Grey with green band and tuft	Black
Light Infantry Volunteer Battalion	Grey	Grey	Grey	Grey	Black	Grey with black tuft	Black
Ouro Arsenal Battalion	Blue	Blue	Black	Blue	Red	Blue with red piping	Natural leather
Craftsman Company of the Ouro Arsenal Battalion	Blue	Blue	Black with frontal white patches	Blue	Black	Blue with black band	White
National Arsenal Battalion	Brown	Brown	Blue	Blue	Black	Brown with blue band	Black

Douro Boatman Battalion	Blue	Blue	Black	Blue	Black	Blue with red piping	White
Ambulance Company	Blue	Blue	Black	Red	Black	Blue with red band	White
National Artillery Battalion	Grey	Grey	Blue	Blue	Black	Grey with blue band	Black
Artillery Company of the 1st Fix/ Garrison Battalion	Grey	Grey	Yellow and red front patches	Grey with black and red piping	Black	Grey	Natural leather
Artillery Company of the 2nd Fix/Garrison Battalion	Grey	Grey	White	Red	Black	Grey with red band	Natural leather
Craftsman Company of the 2nd Fix/Garrison Battalion	Grey	Grey	White	Red	Black	Grey with red band	Natural leather

Miguelite Army

Miguelite Line Units, 1828-34 (Plates 14 to 20)

The Portuguese military organization of this period was effected by the Liberal revolt of 1828 against the absolutist government of. D. Miguel which ended with the defeat of the Liberals and harsh and bloody reprisals, including summary executions and long imprisonment in military fortresses. This episode, the actual beginning of the War of the Two Brothers, was marked by the escape of many Liberal Generals to England aboard the steamship Belfast and the flight of the various regiments to Galicia and thence to England and France. Prior to the 1828 coup, the Miguelite War Office maintained the Peninsular War line unit organisation of 24 infantry regiments (1,552 men each), 12 cavalry regiments (892 men), 12 Caçadores battalions (693 men) and 4 artillery regiments with 4 cart driver companies, 1 corps of engineers and 1 artificer's battalion. This considerable military force, still had many Peninsular War veterans within its ranks. There was another set of second line units forming 54 militia regiments. With the 1828 Liberal revolt and the division of the Portuguese Army into Liberal and Miguelite forces that would be the trigger of the Civil War, the government of D. Miguel, along with taking strong measures to eradicate Liberal ideas and subversive movements, also reorganized the army as follows:

- Line regiments no longer used unit numbers, became attached to permanent barracks and were renamed by the names of the lands of their residence, thus them becoming easier to politically control and watch over.
- Militia regiments were reduced to single battalion's units of five companies: four fusilier's companies and one grenadier company.

- Besides the Militia forces, the Miguelite government raised 40 battalions of Royalist Volunteers which were created to guard and defend the lands of their residence, but they eventually served with the Line Regiments and the Militias.
- The Lisbon Royal Police Guard was reinforced with a force of 3,000 cavalry troopers, infantry and artillerymen becoming a faithful guard of the D. Miguel regime. The Royal Police Guard of Porto continued to exist, though with almost half of the force of Lisbon and always under strong suspicion of Liberal infiltration within their ranks.
- Urban Royalist Volunteer companies were created to guard cities, towns and villages not only from external threats but as internal surveillance units as well.
- The old Ordenança brigades were kept, but much of their troops moved to the Royalist Volunteers, and the remaining troops framed the much feared Miguelite guerrilla bands, famous for their savagery and ruthlessness towards Liberal families or Freemasons.
- Royal Navy Brigade: a marine infantry unit of 1,500 men was kept as a fighting force aboard the Miguelite Navy ships.

Following the Miguelite reorganization, due to the division of the Portuguese Army and the disbanding of several units under the suspicion of Liberal sympathies, in 1829 there were 16 line infantry regiments, four artillery regiments, 4 Caçadores battalions, one engineer and artificers battalion and 48 militia regiments. The number of cavalry regiments was between 10 and 12 units, partially detached to garrison duty in territorial fortresses.

The Miguelite uniforms appear to have remained the same as those of 1815, except for the new shako plate (which apparently only began to be distributed in September 1832). The soldiers may have campaigned in a short white jacket with cuffs and collar, the colour of the regiment as barracks uniforms. The officers would have preferred peaked forage caps, with band in the colour of the regiment, in campaign duties. The distinctive colours of the various regiments and battalions were the same as those used during the Peninsular Wars. The exception seems to be the Caçadores battalions, which had the following colours: black collar and light blue cuffs, for Alentejo Caçadores Battalion (formerly 1st Caçadores Battalion), and light blue collar and cuffs for the Caçadores of Beira Alta Battalion (former 4th Caçadores). Black collar and yellow cuffs for Minho Caçadores (former 7th Caçadores) and light blue collar and black cuffs for Beira Baixa Caçadores (former 8th Caçadores). In 1833, the light blue was changed to green (namely: Alentejo Caçadores' cuffs, Beira Alta Caçadores' green collar and cuffs and Beira Baixa Caçadores Battalion with a green collar).

The new regimental titles retained in service for loyalty to the Miguelite cause were:

Cavalry

- The former 1st Cavalry Regiment became the 1st Cavalry Regiment of Lisbon (barracks in Alcântara),
- The former 4th Cavalry Regiment became the 2nd Lisbon Cavalry Regiment (barracks on the Lisbon area of Ajuda),
- The former 7th Cavalry Regiment became the 3rd Cavalry Regiment of Lisbon (Barracks at Santa Apolónia, close to the Royal Army Arsenal),
- The former 2nd Cavalry Regiment became the Vila Viçosa Cavalry Regiment,
- The former 3rd Cavalry Regiment became the Elvas Cavalry Regiment,
- The former 5th Cavalry Regiment became the Cavalry Regiment of Évora,
- The former 6th and 12th Cavalry Regiments became the Cavalry Regiment of Chaves,
- The former 8th Cavalry Regiment became the Cavalry Regiment of Fundão,

Infantry

- The former 1st Infantry Regiment became the 1st Lisbon Infantry Regiment,
- The former 4th Infantry Regiment became the 2nd Lisbon Infantry Regiment,
- The former 7th Infantry Regiment became the 3rd Lisbon Infantry Regiment,
- The former 16th Infantry Regiment became the Infantry nº16 - 4th Lisbon Infantry Regiment,
- The former 5th Infantry Regiment became the 1st Elvas Infantry Regiment,
- The former 17th Infantry Regiment became the 2nd Elvas Infantry Regiment,
- The former 11th Infantry Regiment became the Almeida Infantry Regiment,
- The former 12th Infantry Regiment became the Chaves Infantry Regiment,
- The former 13th Infantry Regiment became the Infantry Regiment of Leiria,
- The former 14th Infantry Regiment became the Tavira Infantry Regiment,
- The former 19th Infantry Regiment became the Cascais Infantry Regiment,
- The former 20th Infantry Regiment became the Abrantes Infantry Regiment,
- The former 22nd Infantry Regiment became the Infantry Regiment of Valença,
- The former 24th Infantry Regiment became the Bragança Infantry Regiment,

Light Infantry and Caçadores

1st Caçadores Battalion becomes the Alentejo Caçadores Regiment (barracks in Campo Maior),
4th Caçadores Battalion becomes the Beira Alta Caçadores Regiment (barracks in Viseu),
7th Caçadores Battalion becomes the Regiment of Caçadores of Minho (barracks in Guimarães),
8th Caçadores Battalion becomes the Beira Baixa Caçadores Regiment (barracks in Castelo Branco),

Artillery

1st Artillery Regiment becomes the Corte (Lisboa) Artillery Regiment,
2nd Artillery becomes the Faro Artillery Regiment,
3rd Artillery becomes the Elvas Artillery Regiment.

More regiments may have been incorporated into the Miguelite Army. With the evolution of the war, and the rapid shrinkage of Miguelite forces, a final reorganization was implemented, but it was too late to turn the tide.

After the 18 February 1834 (Battle of Almoster), Chief of Staff General João Galvão Mexia de Sousa Mascaren has wanted to '...reduce existing bodies to fractions', thus creating 8 additional infantry regiments, 8 battalions of light Infantry, 4 cavalry regiments and 1 artillery regiment. The existing corps were divided into corps of 200, 250 or 300 men, with new commanders, and the provinces were ordered to send the recruits to Santarém.

Miguelite Militia Regiments, 1828-34 (Plate 21)

In 1793, the former auxiliary troops were reorganized and retitled militias. In the the army organization of 1806, the country was divided into 3 Territorial Military Divisions, in turn divided into 24 recruiting districts. Each of these districts corresponded to 1 first line infantry regiment, 2 militia regiments, and 1 Ordenança brigade. During the D. Miguel Regency, 1828-34, militia regiments were reduced to battalions of 6 companies. The organization of Militia Regiments was retained during the civil war, with units on either side, but the majority maintained loyalty to the Miguelite government. In addition, some non-integrated regiments were created. Thus, there were the following militia units:

Northern Division Militias:
Bragança Militia Regiment
Chaves Militia Regiment
Miranda Militia Regiment
Vila Real Militia Regiment
Arches Militia Regiment
Barca Militia Regiment
Barcelos Militia Regiment
Basto Militia Regiment
Braga Militia Regiment
Guimarães Militia Regiment
Viana Militia Regiment
Vila do Conde Militia Regiment
Feira Militia Regiment
Maia Militia Regiment
Penafiel Militia Regiment
Porto Militia Regiment
Center Division Militias
Alcácer do Sal Militia Regiment
Leiria Militia Regiment
Lousã Militia Regiment
Santarém Militia Regiment
Setúbal Militia Regiment
Soure Militia Regiment
Torres Vedras Militia Regiment
Court of the West Side Militia Regiment (Lisbon)
Court of the East Side Militia Regiment (Lisbon)
Royal Volunteer Regiment of West Lisbon Foot Militias
Royal Volunteer Regiment of East Lisbon Foot Militias
Coimbra Militia Regiment
Aveiro Militia Regiment
Figueira da Foz Militia Regiment
Oliveira de Azeméis Militia Regiment
Southern Division Militias
Avis Militia Regiment
Beja Militia Regiment

Évora Militia Regiment
Portalegre Militia Regiment
Vila Viçosa Militia Regiment
Lagos Militia Regiment
Tavira Militia Regiment
Arganil Militia Regiment
Arouca Militia Regiment
Castelo Branco Militia Regiment
Covilhã Militia Regiment
Guard Militia Regiment
Idanha-a-Nova Militia Regiment
Lamego Militia Regiment
Tondela Militia Regiment
Trancoso Militia Regiment
Viseu Militia Regiment
Non Divisionary Independent Militia Units
Royal Horse Militia Volunteer Regiment
Royal Volunteers of Commerce Cavalry Regiment
Royal Volunteer of Commerce Infantry Regiment
East Lisbon National Artilleryman Battalion
West Lisbon National Gunners Battalion
East Lisbon National Caçadores Battalion
Western Lisbon National Caçadores Battalion
Royal Volunteers Battalion of Porto

Miguelite Royalist Volunteers (Plate 22)

The Corps of Royalist Volunteers was a Portuguese militia organization created by D. Miguel I to defend the absolute monarchy against Liberal ideas of former Emperor Pedro I of Brazil, briefly D. Pedro IV King of Portugal, and D. Pedro of Bragança, regent in the name of his daughter, Queen Dona Maria II. The corps was created by decree on 26 May 1828 following the failed Liberal revolt in Porto. Its appointed commander was D. Nuno Caetano Alvares Pereira de Melo, 6th Duke of Cadaval, a radical absolutist.

Within the Miguelite army, the Corps of Royalist Volunteers was an elite echelon of the kingdom militias and, unlike the latter, consisting only of volunteers specially selected from supporters of the 'Realist' cause. They were Miguelite shock troops, and as violent and blood-thirsty as anticipated. It was initially predicted that the corps would only consist of two brigades stationed in Lisbon, each with two battalions. Subsequent to this, in the face of a large supply of volunteers, 48 battalions were raised across the country, many of them as light infantry or Caçadores units. Information about the uniforms of these battalions is scarce and dispersed, but it is likely that attire and equipment would closely follow army and militia regiments with dark blue coats for infantry, cavalry and artillery and blue and brown for light infantry or Caçadores.

With the constitution of the Miguelist government in 1828, the first special military measures were taken, notably the dissolution of the Liberal Volunteer Commerce battalions and the National Guards of Lisbon and the creation of the corps of Royalist Volunteers as second line troops, alongside the militia regiments. On 26 May, the first battalions were formed in Lisbon, forming a corps of 2,000 men whose command was taken by D. Miguel himself. Other battalions were formed in different areas of the country, namely Minho, Trás-os-Montes, Beiras, Alentejo and Algarve, for a total of 49 battalions. On 10 July 1832, D. Pedro and the Liberal government ordered the disbandment of Royalist volunteer battalions that he accused of being illegally organized. National battalions were created in their place. These units were permanently disbanded following the Liberal victory in 1834.

The Corps of Royalist volunteers took an active part in the war, especially after confrontations became widespread throughout the country. Even after the civil war ended, some members of the corps continued to fight as guerrillas. See list below for territorial growth of the Royalist volunteers:

Kingdom of Algarve
Battalion of Royalist Volunteers of Tavira
Alentejo Province
Battalion of Royalist Volunteers of Beja
Battalion of Royalist Volunteers of Elvas
Battalion of Royalist Volunteers of Évora
Battalion of Royalist Volunteers of Moura
Battalion of Royalist Volunteers of Monsaraz
Battalion of Royalist Volunteers of Portalegre
Battalion of Royalist Volunteers of Serpa
Battalion of Royalist Volunteers of Vila Viçosa
Cavalry Company of Royalist Volunteers of Monforte
Estremadura Province
1st Brigade of Royalist Volunteers
1st Battalion of Lisbon Royalist Volunteers
2nd Battalion of Lisbon Royalist Volunteers
1st Cavalry Company of Lisbon Royalist Volunteers
2nd Brigade of Royalist Volunteers
3rd Battalion of Lisbon Royalist Volunteers
4th Battalion de Volunteers Royalists de Lisboa
2nd Cavalry Company of Lisbon Royalist Volunteers
Battalion of Royalist Volunteers of Santarém
Battalion of Royalist Volunteers of Sintra
Battalion of Royalist Volunteers of Tomar
Battalion of Royalist Volunteers of Torres Vedras

Caçadores Company of Royalist Volunteers of Alenquer
Caçadores Company of Volunteers of Leiria
Caçadores Company of Volunteers of Samora Correia
Lancers Company of Royalist Volunteers of Salvaterra de Magos
Beira Baixa Province
Battalion of Royalist Volunteers of Castelo Branco
Battalion of Royalist Volunteers of Covilhão and Fundão
Battalion of Royalist Volunteers of Penamacor
Beira Alta Province
Battalion of Royalist Volunteers of Arganil
Battalion of Royalist Volunteers of Castro Daire
Battalion of Royalist Volunteers of Guarda
Battalion of Royalist Volunteers of Lamego
Battalion of Royalist Volunteers of Mangualde
Battalion of Royalist Volunteers of Trancoso
Caçadores Company of Volunteers of Vale de Besteiros
Porto Military District
Battalion of Royalist Volunteers of Aveiro
Battalion of Royalist Volunteers of Oliveira de Azeméis
Battalion of Royalist Volunteers of Penafiel
Entre-Douro-e-Minho Province
Battalion of Royalist Volunteers of Barcelos
Battalion of Royalist Volunteers of Braga
Battalion of Royalist Volunteers of Guimarães
Battalion of Royalist Volunteers of Viana do Castelo
Trás-os-Montes Province
Battalion of Royalist Volunteers of Chaves
Battalion of Royalist Volunteers of Mirandela
Battalion of Royalist Volunteers of Montalegre
Battalion of Royalist Volunteers of Vila Flor
Battalion of Royalist Volunteers of Vila Real

Naval Forces

Liberal Navy

D. Pedro, on arrival in Europe, visited the French and British courts. His aim was to gather support for his cause, both political and military. He was struggling with serious financial problems at this time. One of the most important and urgent steps was to raise a credible fighting force and to have a navy large enough to engage a hostile naval squadron and a respectable fleet of transport ships. This was a most complex and difficult task, especially concerning the combat fleet. D. Pedro and his staff were well aware of the power of D. Miguel's fleet despite the accelerating decline of the Portuguese Navy since the Peninsular War. Indeed, the loss of some ships of the line, retained in Brazil after independence and, on 11 July 1831, the seizure of part of the Portuguese fleet by French Admiral Roussin following a diplomatic incident with the D. Miguel government, contributed to the naval decline. D. Pedro left his wife and Dona Maria in Paris, went to Belle Isle, where he embarked with troops aboard his new fleet for the Island of Terceira. On 10 February 1832, D. Pedro sailed from Belle Isle for the Azores with a fleet, composed of the frigates *Rainha de Portugal* and *D. Maria II*, corvette *Amélia*, schooner *Terceira*, and troop transport, *Eugénia*. Liberal forces from Terceira island undertook the occupation of the entire Azores archipelago. For this, a naval squadron was essential. There, he also obtained the services of Captain George Sartorius, who volunteered to command the Queen's naval forces, and various English officers. From Brazil he already had the corvette *Regência de Portugal*, which he had acquired in Rio de Janeiro, and the schooner *Boa Esperança*, which was offered to him in the same place. With him also came the brig *Conde de Vila Flor*, the former *D. Estevão de Ataíde*, requested by the Consul of Portugal for the cause of D. Maria II. On 22 February 1832, the former emperor disembarked at Ponta Delgada. The force of 8,300 men gathered in the Azores was now ready to sail for the continent in a convoy of 42 transport ships under the protection of the assembled fleet. Political divisions amongst the Liberals led D. Pedro to undertake a most important task, which was to conciliate many ideologically divided Liberal supporters. This subsequently brought him into collision with the then Admiral George Rose Sartorius. Later, he was replaced by Admiral Charles Napier.

Admiral Sir Charles Napier, Count of St. Vincent. (National Library of Portugal)

On 20 June 1832, D. Pedro left the Azores with 42 ships under the protection of the fleet commanded by Admiral Sartorius. It was composed of the frigate *Rainha de Portugal*, bearing the admiral's flag, with 46 guns (commanded by Captain Crosbie); the frigate *Dona Maria II*, with 42 guns (commanded by Captain Mins); the corvette *Amélia* with 24 guns (commanded by Captain Bertram), D. Pedro was onboard the latter; the brigs *Villa-Flor* with 16 guns and *Terceira* with 7 guns, *Coquette* with 7 guns, the *Liberal* with 9 guns; the *Boa Esperança* and *Eugenia* both with 10 guns, and some schooners, primarily manned by English sailors. The expedition arrived at Vila do Conde on the 7 July and the fleet was at anchor in the Bay of Mindelo up to Arnosa de Pampelido, 14 km from Porto on the 8th. For the Liberal forces heading to Porto, a long and difficult journey overland began. There having been for a short period of time, a naval blockade to Lisbon, D. Miguel gave orders to his naval squadron to leave the Tagus, this time with the stated purpose of fighting the enemy. Miguelite Admiral Pereira de Campos left the Tagus bar in September and headed north. The first engagement finally took place oof Vigo on 11 October 1832, The fight was intense, but the result inconclusive, with no major damage to either side. By this time, there was already serious dissension between Sartorius and the commander of the frigate *Dona Maria II,* Captain Mins, coupled with late payments. This degenerated into an open garrison revolt, with a mutiny of about 200 English sailors who refused to obey direct orders. This occurred when it was crucial that transport ships maintain the supply route and when it was necessary to provide support with naval gunfire support against Miguelite artillery batteries situated at the bar of the Douro. This was essential, as the hostile guns were incessantly bombarding in the city, and almost interdicted the river bar. The smaller warships, boldly patrolling into the Douro river to provide fire support, were thus systematically sunk. So it was that the D. Pedro's fleet lost two brigs and two schooners. Despite the arrival of fleet reinforcements, a 50-gun heavy frigate, the *D. Pedro*, purchased in England with funds raised by friends of the Queen's cause, political intrigues amongst the Liberal command became very serious. Thus, D. Pedro's government began to seriously consider replacing Sartorius. This resulted in discussions with Scottish Captain Charles Napier. He would go on to command the entire Liberal fleet until the end of the civil war.

Liberal fleet (George Sartorius and Charles Napier)

Fifth Rate Great Frigate *Rainha de Portugal* with 46 guns, acting flagship, under the command of Commodore Wilkinson and Captain MacDonough
Fifth Rate Great Frigate *Dona Maria II* with 42 guns, under the command of Captain Peake
Fifth Rate Great Frigate *D. Pedro* with 50 guns, under the command of Captain Thomas Goble. This frigate was augmented to the squadron during the Siege of Porto, not present at the landing of D. Pedro's Army in 8th July 1832.
Unrated Corvette *Vila Flor* with 18 guns, under the command of Acting Captain Ruxton.
Unrated Brig *Portuense* with 20 guns under the command of Acting Captain Blackstone.
Unrated Schooner *Faro* with 6 guns
A small force of steam tugs and a considerable fleet of transports

Plate 1 Liberal Army Line Units 1832-1834

D. Pedro in 5th Caçadores
Batt. Colonel undress uniform

Marshal Saldanha in
Army full dress uniform

Bernardo de Sá Nogueira
Baron of Sá da Bandeira
10th Infantry undress uniform

Colonel of 18th Infantry
Campaign uniform

Colonel of 6th Infantry
Campaign uniform

Lieutenant of 18th Infantry
undress uniform

Lieutenant of 2nd Caçadores
Batt. Campaign uniform

Lieutenant 3rd Caçadores
Batt. undress uniform

Plate 2 Liberal Army Line Units 1832-1834

Private/Officer of the Sacred Battalion

1st Sergeant 18th Infantry Regiment Grenadier Coy.

Corporal 6th Infantry Regiment Fusilier Coy.

Private 10th Infantry Regiment Fusilier Coy.

Private 18th Infantry Regiment rear view and full gear

2nd Sergeant 2nd Caçadores Batt.

Corporal 3rd Caçadores Batt.

Private 5th Caçadores Batt.

Plate 3 Liberal Army Line Units 1832-1834

2nd Sergeant
10th Cavalry Regiment

Private
11th Cavalry Regiment

Private
10th Cavalry Regiment
rear view

Captain
11th Cavalry Regiment
undress uniform with cape

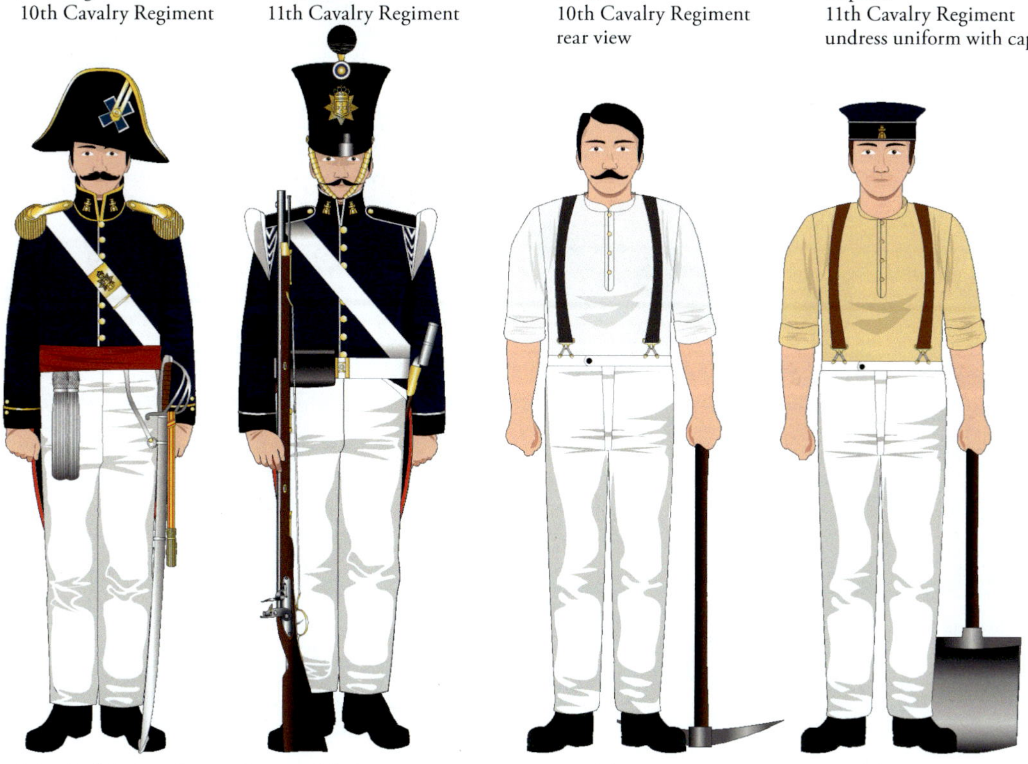

Colonel of the Royal
Engineers Corps

Private of the Engineer
Battalion of Artificers

Sapper of the Engineer
Battalion of Artificers

Sapper of the Engineer
Battalion of Artificers

Plate 4 Liberal Army Line Units 1832-1834

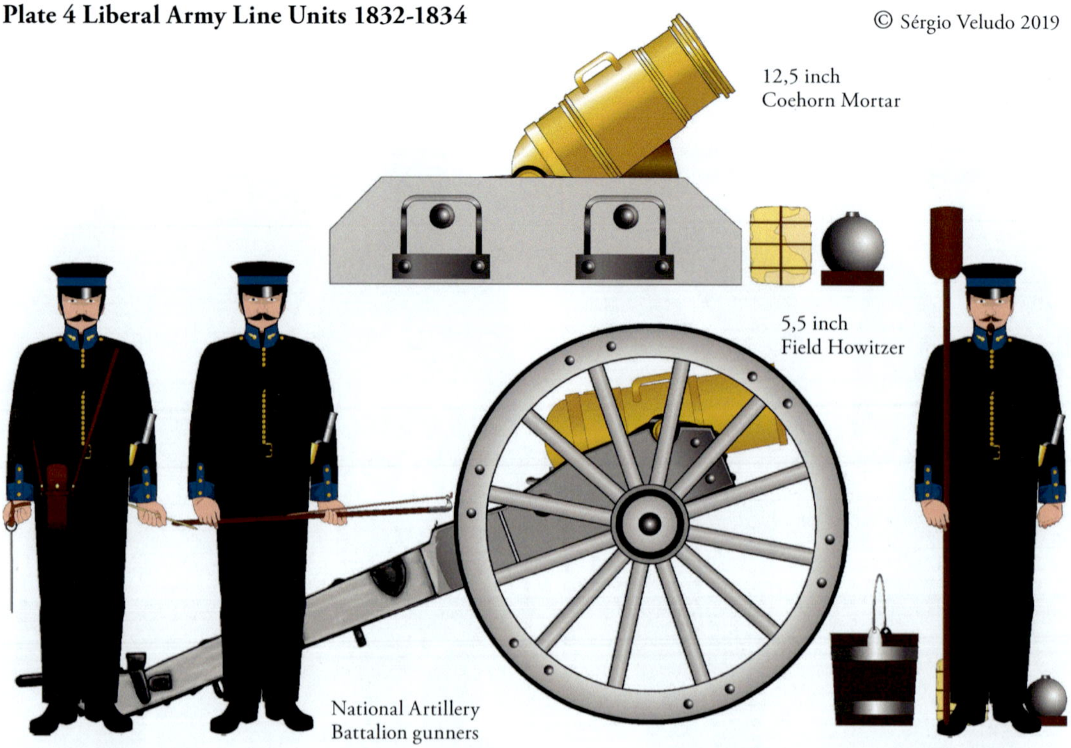

Plate 5 Liberal Army Line Units 1832-1834

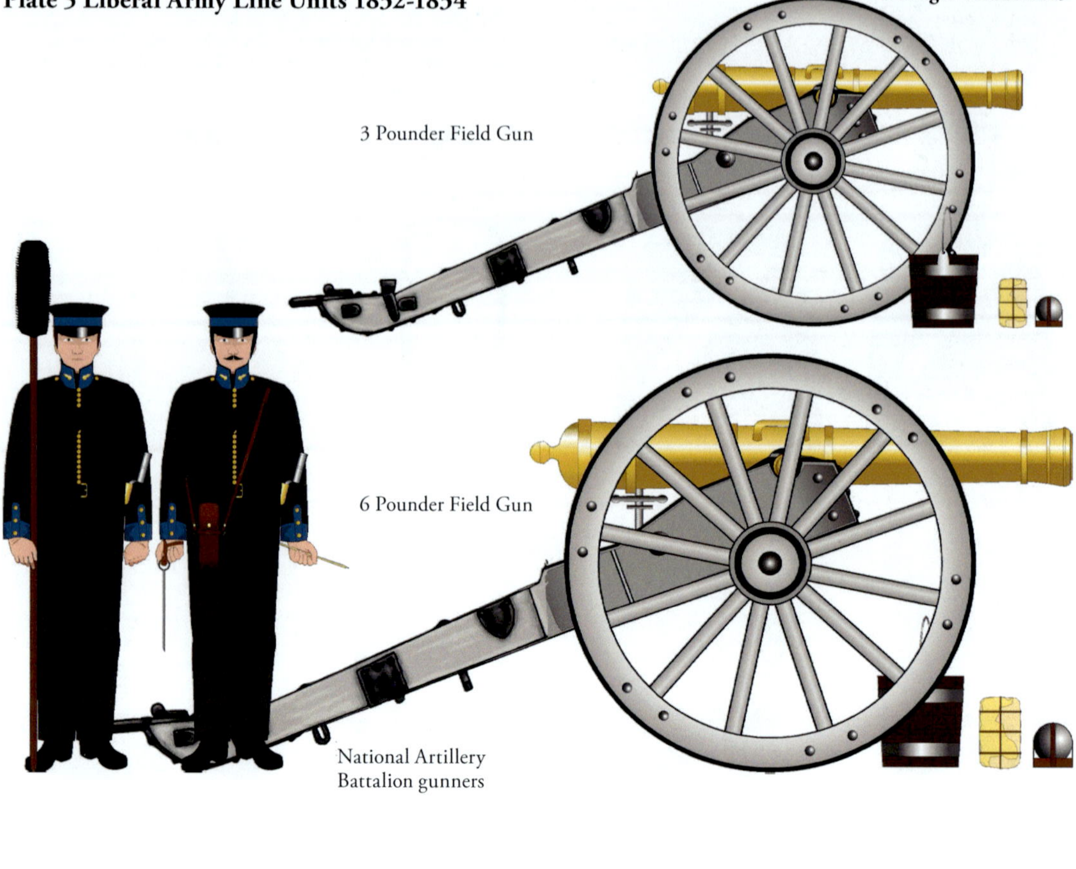

Plate 6 Liberal Army Line Units 1832-1834

Ensign 18th
Infantry Regiment
Constitutional Colours

Drummer 6th
Infantry Regiment
Fusilier Coy.

Ensign 10th
Infantry Regiment
Battle Flag

Plate 7 Liberal Army Foreign Troops 1832-1834
Belgians, French and Italians

Belgian Tirailleur
Corps

Belgian Tirailleur
Corps Light Company

Belgian Tirailleur
Corps Light Company

Portuguese Tirailleurs
French fusilier

Portuguese Tirailleurs
French fusilier

Portuguese Tirailleurs
Italian rifleman

Portuguese Tirailleurs
French fusilier (rear view)

Portuguese Tirailleurs
Officer in French uniform

Plate 8 Liberal Army Foreign Troops 1832-1834
British, Irish and Scottish

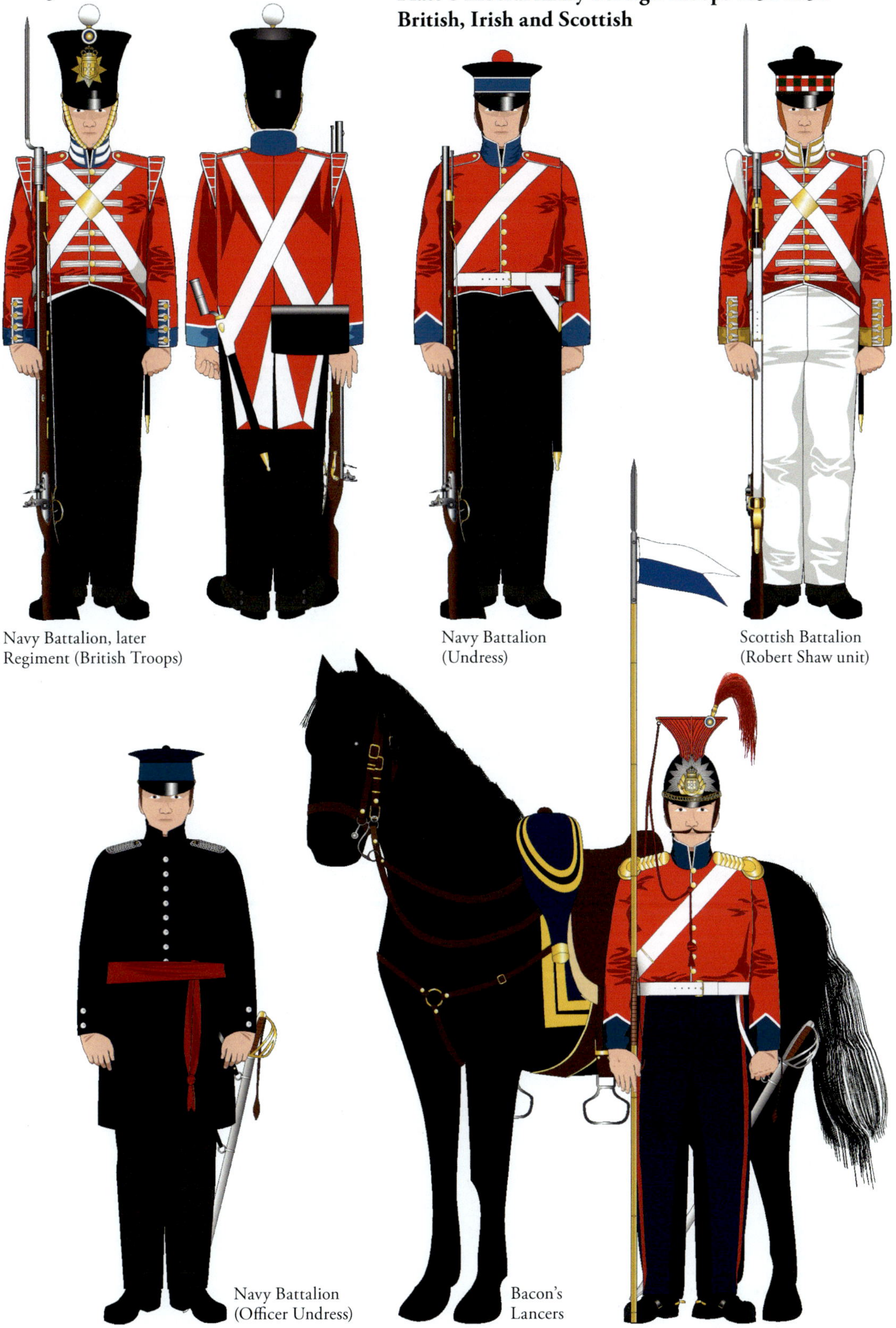

Navy Battalion, later Regiment (British Troops)

Navy Battalion (Undress)

Scottish Battalion (Robert Shaw unit)

Navy Battalion (Officer Undress)

Bacon's Lancers

Plate 9 Liberal Army Foreign Troops 1832-1834 British, Irish and Scottish

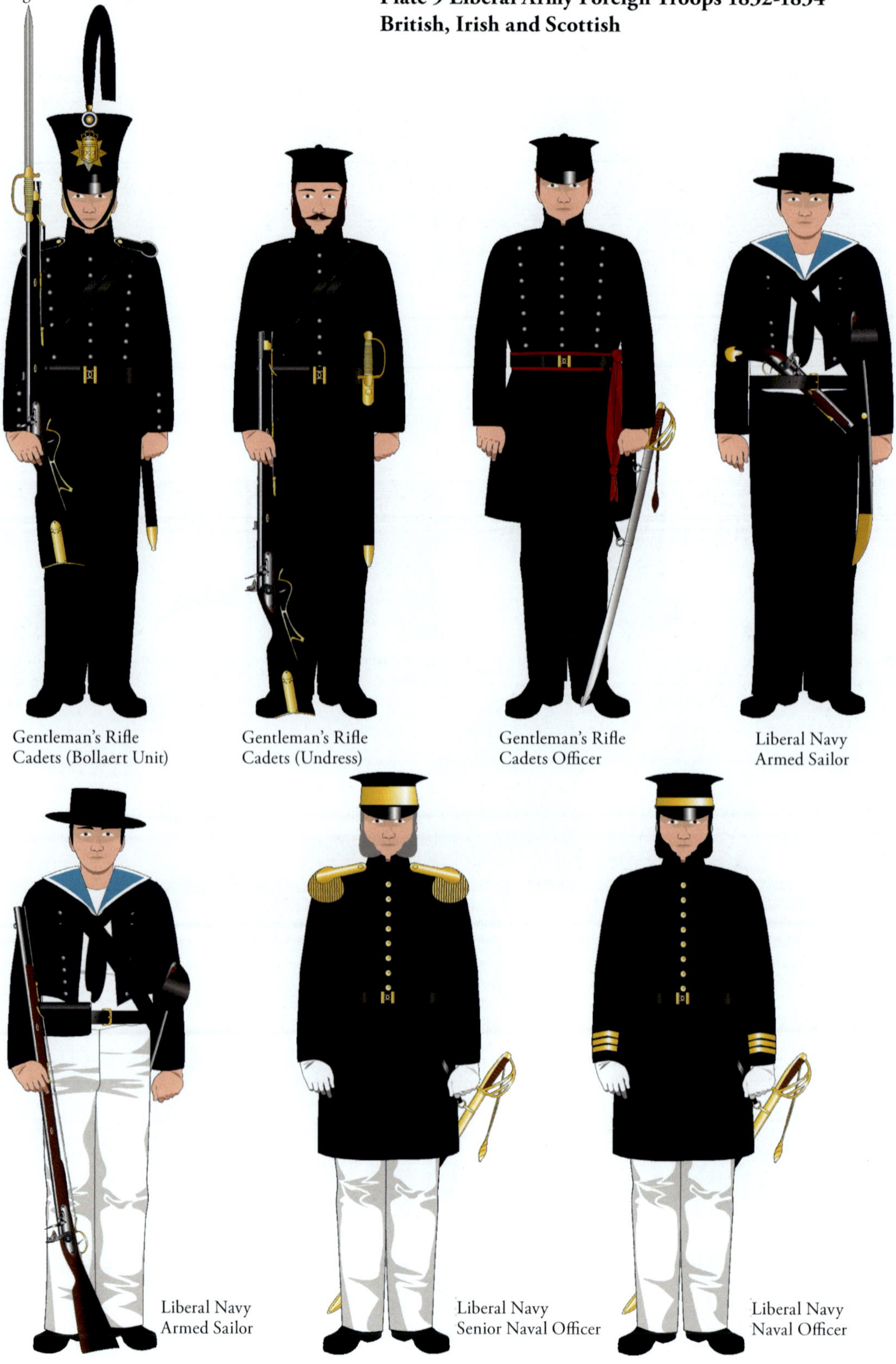

Plate 10 Liberal Army Volunteer National Battalions 1832-1834

Artillery Company
1st Fix/Garrison Battalion

Artillery Company
2nd Fix/Garrison Battalion

Artillery Company
2nd Fix/Garrison Battalion

Queen's Own Volunteers
rear view

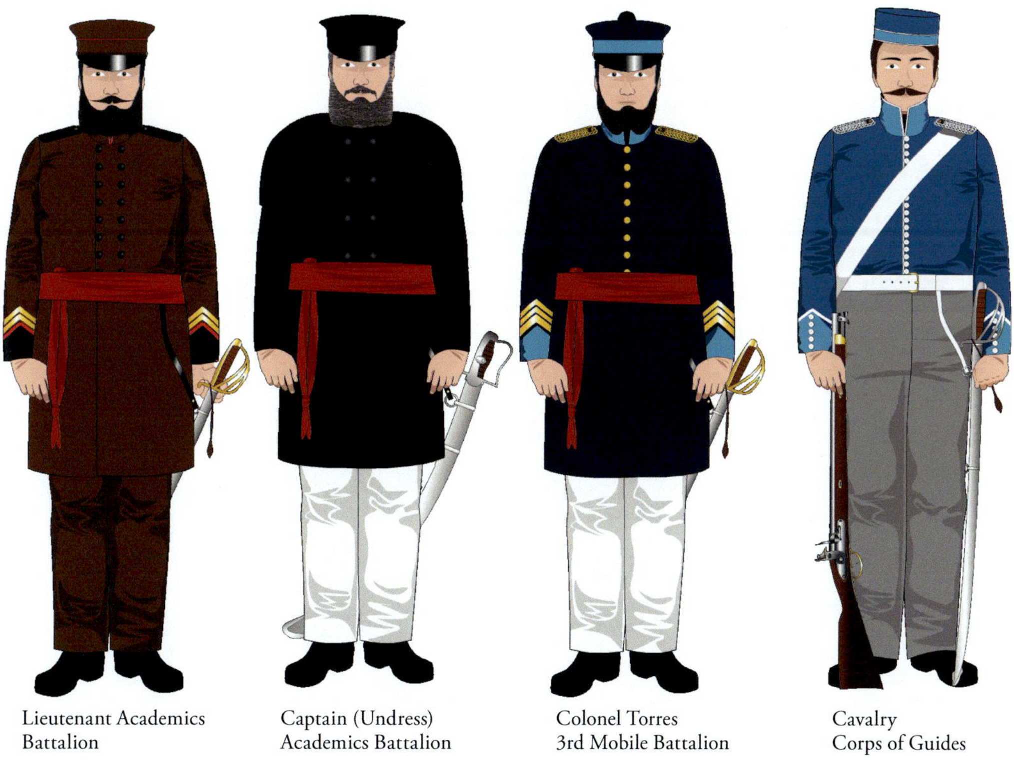

Lieutenant Academics
Battalion

Captain (Undress)
Academics Battalion

Colonel Torres
3rd Mobile Battalion

Cavalry
Corps of Guides

Plate 11 Liberal Army Volunteer National Battalions 1832-1834

Academics Battalion | Queen's Own Volunteers | 1st Mobile Battalion | 2nd Mobile Battalion

3rd Mobile Battalion | 1st Fix/Garrison Battalion | 2nd Fix/Garrison Battalion | 1st Provisional Battalion of Santa Catarina

Plate 12 Liberal Army Volunteer National Battalions 1832-1834

2nd Provisional Battalion of Santa Ovidio

3rd Provisional Battalion of Cedofeita

Craftsman Company 1st Fix Battalion

Lampion Keepers Company

Public Employees Battalion

Beira Baixa Battalion

Beira Alta Battalion

Trás os Montes Battalion

Plate 13 Liberal Army Volunteer National Battalions 1832-1834

Minho Battalion

Light Infantry Volunteer Battalion

Ouro Arsenal Battalion

Craftsman Company Ouro Arsenal Battalion

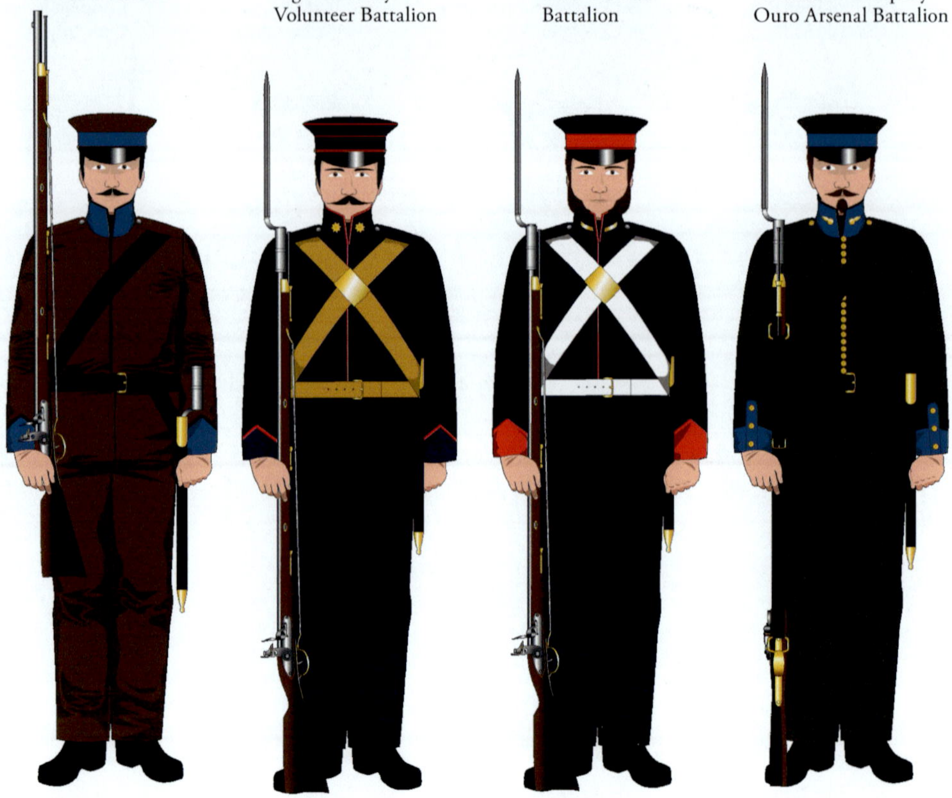

National Arsenal Battalion

Douro Boatman Battalion

Ambulances Company

National Artillery Battalion

Plate 14 Miguelite Army Line Units 1832-1834

D. Miguel of Bragança
Commander in Chief of
the Miguelite Army

General Álvaro Xavier
Póvoas in Army
full dress uniform

General in Army
full dress uniform
rear view

General Santa Marte
in Field Uniform

Colonel of 1st Infantry
Regiment or 1st Lisbon
Infantry Regiment

Colonel of 11th Infantry
Regiment or Almeida
Infantry Regiment

Captain of 12th Infantry
Regiment or Chaves Infantry
Regiment Undress Uniform

Plate 15 Miguelite Army Line Units 1832-1834

Priv. 24th Infantry Regiment or Bragança Infantry Regiment

Priv. 24th Infantry Regiment or Bragança Infantry Regiment rear view

Priv. 22nd Infantry Regiment or Valença Infantry Regiment in white shell jacket

Lieutenant of 7nd Caçadores Batt. or Minho Caçadores Batt.

Lieutenant of 7nd Caçadores Batt. or Minho Caçadores Batt. rear view

Corporal 11th Caçadores Batt.

Private 8th Caçadores Batt. or Beira Baixa Caçadores Batt. Undress uniform

Plate 16 Miguelite Army Line Units 1832-1834

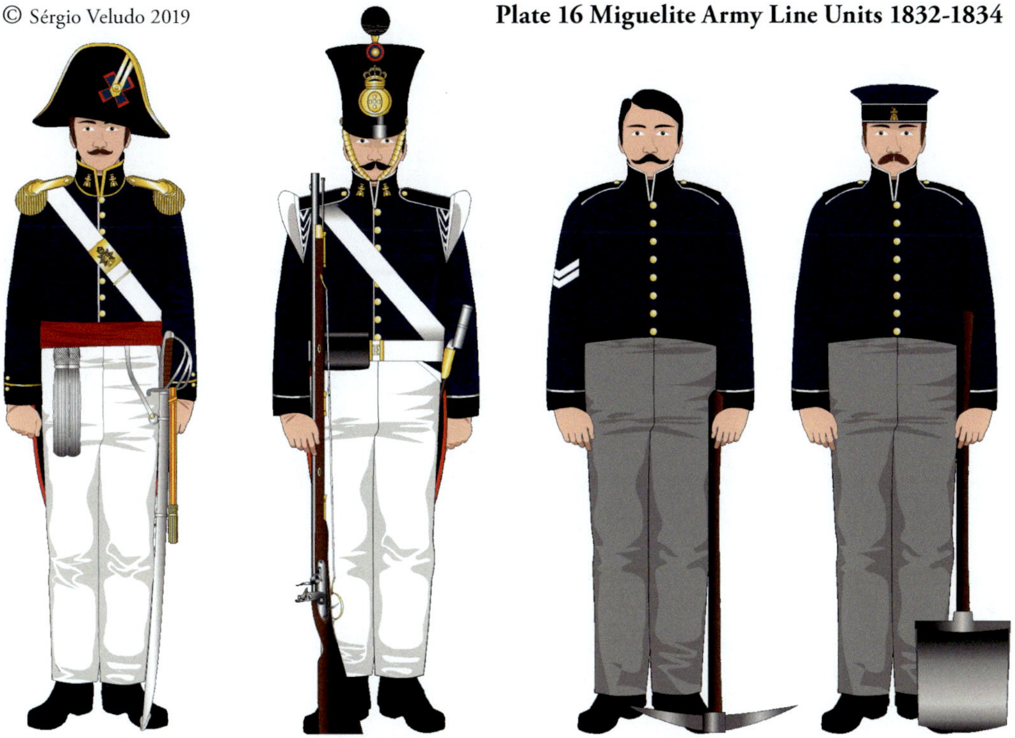

Colonel of the Royal Engineers Corps

Private of the Engineer Battalion of Artificers

Sappers of the Engineer Battalion of Artificers

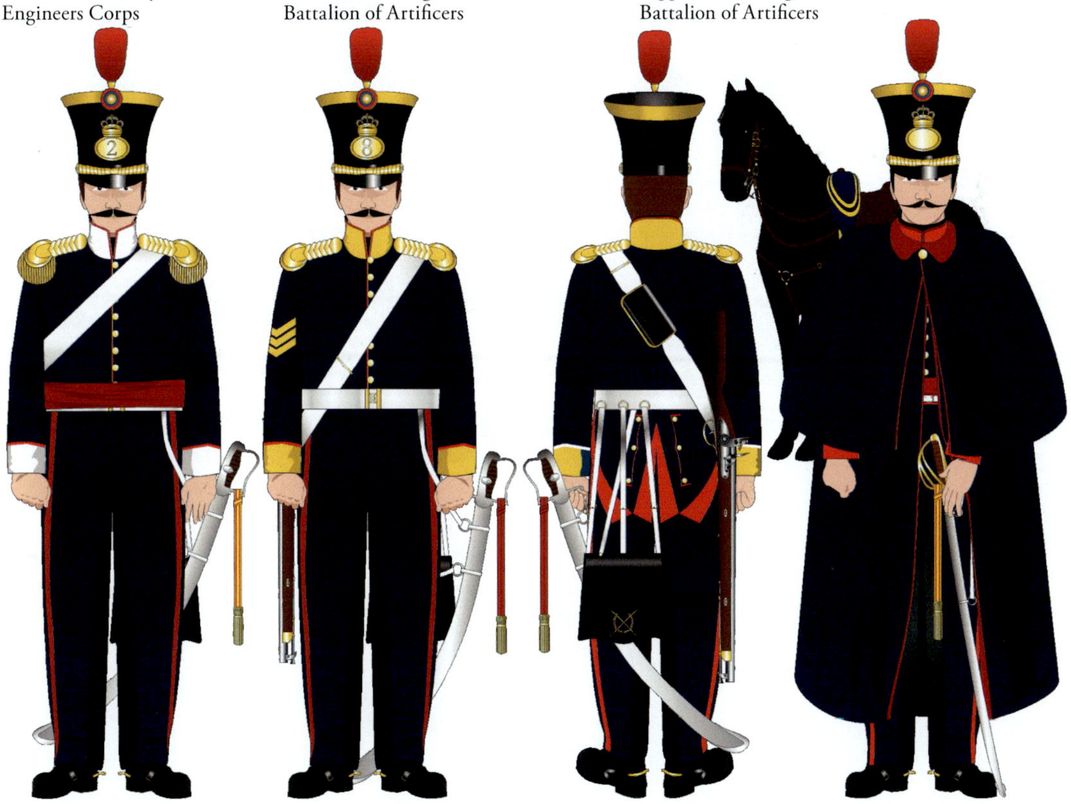

Captain 2nd Lisbon Cavalry Regiment

2nd Sergeant 8th Cavalry Regiment (Fundão)

2nd Sergeant 8th Cavalry Regiment (Fundão) rear view

Captain 5th Cavalry Regiment (Évora) Undress uniform with cape

Plate 17 Miguelite Army Line Units 1832-1834

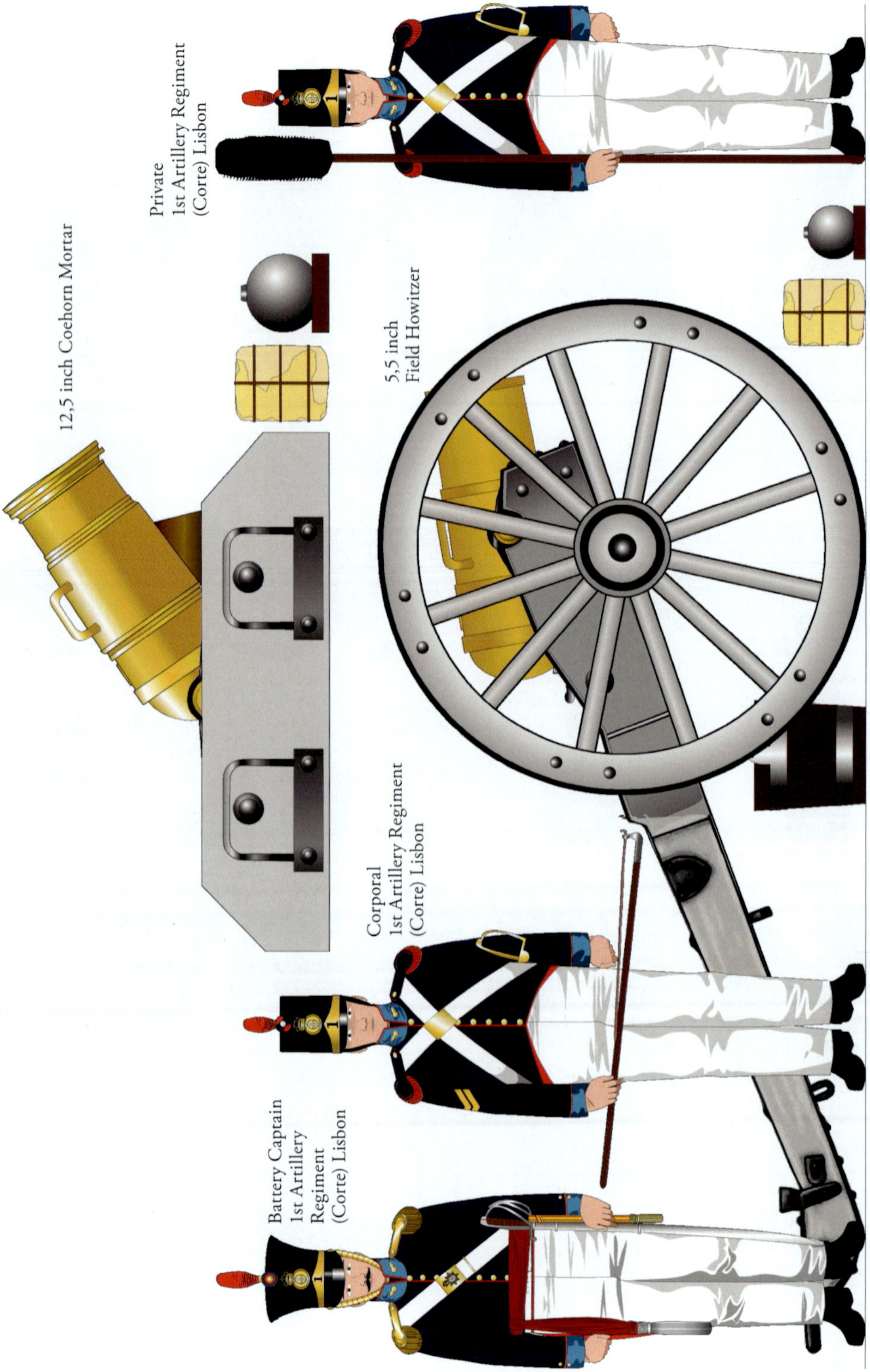

Plate 18 Miguelite Army Line Units 1832-1834

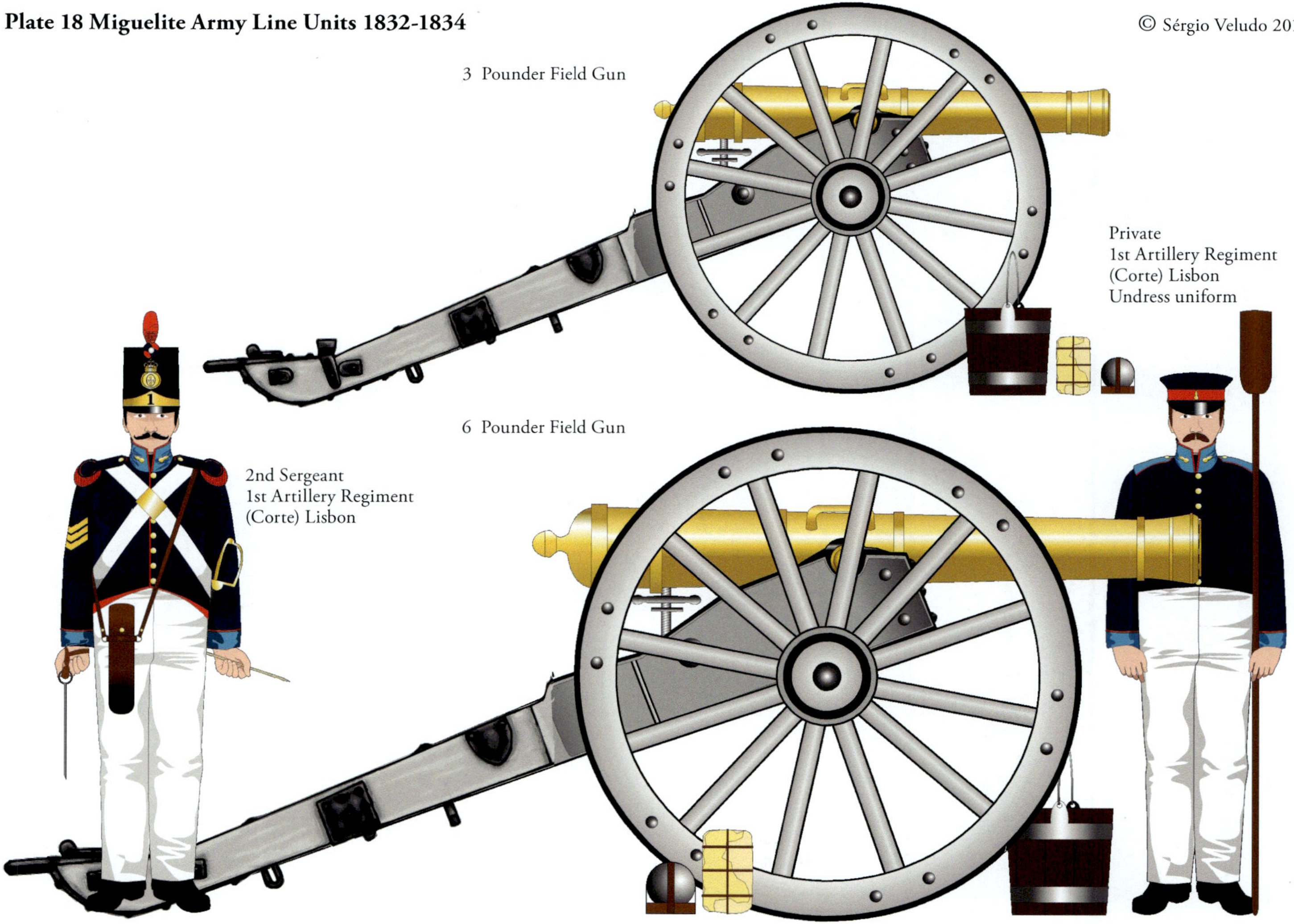

Plate 19 Miguelite Army Line Units 1832-1834

Plate 20 Miguelite Army Line Units 1832-1834

Ensign 1st Infantry Regiment (Lisbon) Miguelite Colours

Drummer 1st Infantry Regiment Fusilier Coy.

Ensign 19th Infantry Regiment Battle Flag

Plate 21 Miguelite Army Militia, Volunteer and Navy Units 1832-1834

Colonel Militia Regiment of Penafiel

Captain Militia Regiment of Guimarães

Captain Militia Regiment of Braga

Captain Royal Police Guard of Lisbon (Cavalry)

Private Royal Police Guard of Lisbon (Infantry)

Corporal Militia Regiment of Maia

Private Militia Regiment of Vila do Conde

Plate 22 Miguelite Militia, Volunteer and Navy Units 1832-1834

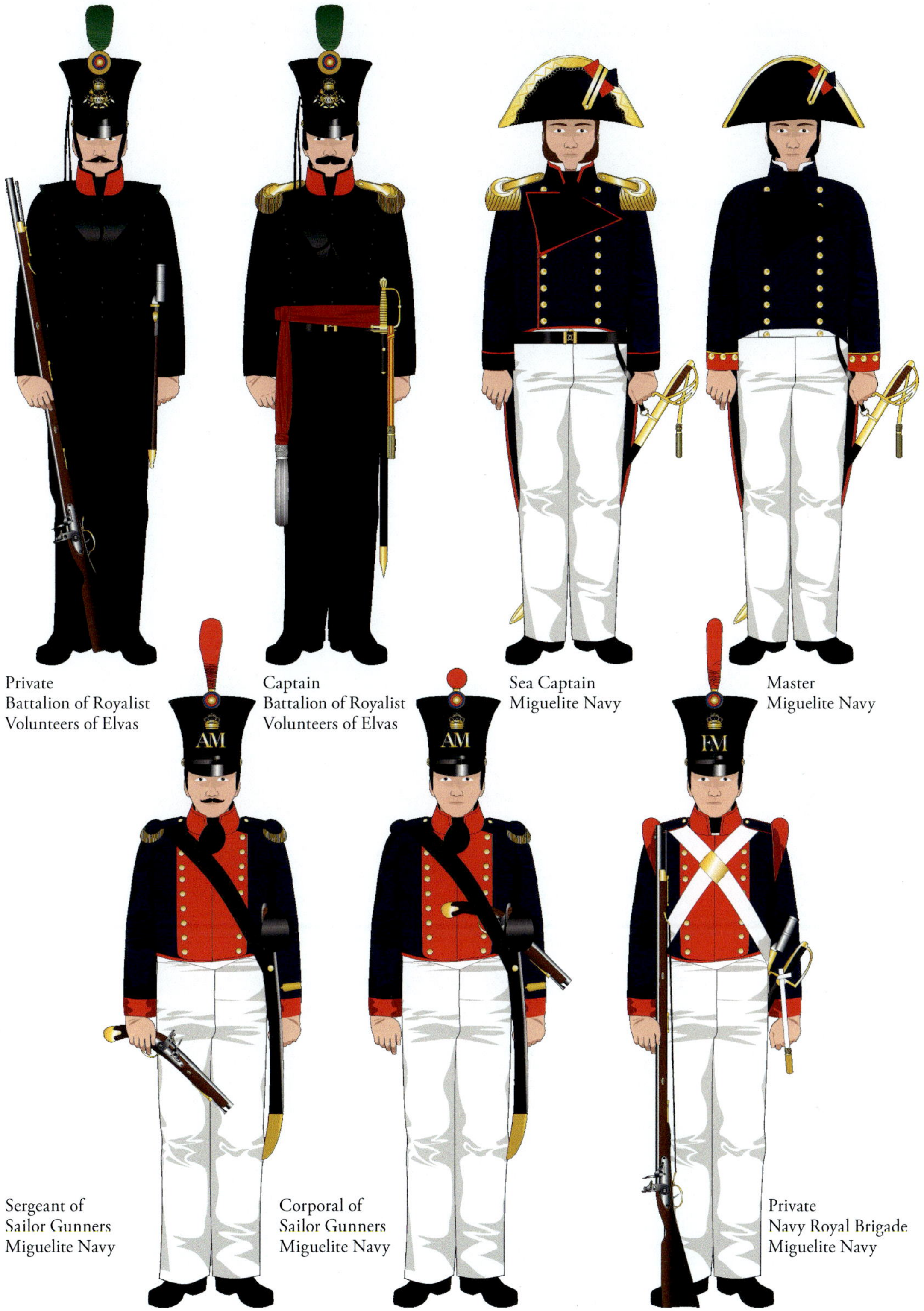

Private
Battalion of Royalist
Volunteers of Elvas

Captain
Battalion of Royalist
Volunteers of Elvas

Sea Captain
Miguelite Navy

Master
Miguelite Navy

Sergeant of
Sailor Gunners
Miguelite Navy

Corporal of
Sailor Gunners
Miguelite Navy

Private
Navy Royal Brigade
Miguelite Navy

Santarém 1834. (S.P. Lohia Collection)

Liberal Marine Troops (Plate 9)

In London in the autumn of 1831, the Liberals bought ships and began to open offices in surrounding parishes for the recruitment of men for land and sea service. Although only 400 men were available (instead of the intended 1,200 men), they formed the initial core of the Navy or British Battalion. Undercover Miguelite efforts and subversive actions led to the withdrawal of 150 men. The 350-ton transport *Edward*, was chartered to carry the remaining 250 men. On 14 December 1831, it was moored off Deptford. She subsequently sailed for Belle-Isle, arriving there in early 1832 where recruitment continued. At Belle-Isle on 20 January 1832, George Hodges assumed command of this regiment, after which he made uniform, armament, and equipment acquisitions and obtained 150 battle-hardened veterans who would also serve as frigate and schooner crewmen. Some 60 marines and 1 ensign of the frigate *Rainha de Portugal* and 40 marines and 1 ensign of the frigate *Dona Maria II* were assigned. Fifty more were distributed to other vessels. The remaining 200 (neither uniformed, equipped or armed) were under the command of Major Williams aboard the transport ship *Edward*. On 5 February, fidelity to the Queen was sworn and the flag was handed over to the battalion. At the time of departure for the Azores there were already a 500 marines, still mostly '... undisciplined, unarmed and naked'. The careers and occupations were quite heterogeneous: the late king's hairdresser, comics, songwriters, chimney sweeps, boxers, office clerks, medical students, painters, printers, and poets. There were also several former soldiers. On 10 of February, the squadron sailed foe the Azores. On 1 March, they left Angra do Heroísmo for Vila da Praia. On 9 March, a schooner with '... clothes, weapons and equipment', arrived from England. On the 27th, they boarded the *Borodino* transport, which arrived on the 29 of March at S. Miguel island to be subsequently landed at Ponta Delgada. These corps participated in the landings in Mindelo and participated in several actions during the Siege of Porto. The Decree of 31 October 1832 created the Armada (Navy) Regiment of 4 battalions. After the battle of S. Vicente, the troops of the Miguelite Navy Royal Regiment were also integrated. This brigade accompanied Admiral Napier on his northern conquests between late 1833 and 1834 (Caminha, etc., etc.).

This naval battalion was recruited in England and was intended for permanent service on frigates and schooners and ground operations in a way very much akin to the British Royal Marines. At Belle-Isle in January 1832, only 150 men aboard the frigates and schooners were in uniform, armed with flintlock India Pattern muskets and equipment. The remaining 200 men would receive uniforms upon their arrival in the Azores. On 21 January 1832, two schooners arrived with, among other things, '... red uniforms, jackets and cloaks for 800 foreigners.'

The frigate *Rainha de Portugal* honour guard that welcomed D. Pedro and the squadron officers on 2 February 1832, consisted of 60 of 150 marines that are described as '... of excellent appearance and excellently armed and uniformed as never before in their British Majesty's navy frigates.' However, in Vila da Praia, Azores in early 1832, the men were still 'miserably dressed' and, in some cases, 'barefoot'. An oft-mentioned issue with this corps was drunkenness that resulted in members selling shirts and boots in exchange for drinking money. During the Army general inspection in Ponta Delgada of 6 June 1832 when the battalion was the only one not to form in 'white pants'. Some of the auxiliary units disembarked on the beaches of Pampelido, '... with long uniforms of the English and French standards of that time, and infantry-like barretinas.' The uniforms apparently had '... overlapping breastplates and two cufflinks.' The shako plates '... were of star shape ... the fins, bow and plume were of the same arrangement as those of the army.' They always carried uncovered shakos despite general distribution of oilskin protective covers. ms. Hodges observed on 29 September 1832 that his troops' muskets were not the best and would warm up to such an extent that with '...incessant use their handling became dangerous.' For this reason, he ordered 200 new muskets and ammunition (for 210 men) from the depot. On the 19 January 1833, during a siege of Porto general inspection, they were described as '...portraits of falstaff troops.' Dressed in rags and tatters, some with "*no pants*", few with 'shoes and socks'; 'some in uniform', others only partially. Others still had their shako and were armed with muskets and bayonets without sheaths. Later, already in Lisbon in February 1834, a beggar is described as wearing an '...old red jacket, anchor buttons, blue Tower ribbon and sword on his chest, and cable lines on his arm.' He was former regimental corporal Thomas Knight, who wrote a work on the subject.

Miguelite Navy

The Portuguese Navy stagnated and rotted in the Brazilian harbours during the royal court exile in Brazil, between 1807 and 1821. The inactivity, poor maintenance and extreme tropical climate degraded the fleet. Moreover, Portuguese ships of the line sheltering in the Brazilian ports ensured the squadron was removed from the European fighting. This suited British interests and strengthened its naval power in such a way as to prevent any aid, and neutralize allied navies challenging Albion's supremacy of the seas. This might be overstatement, but it is important to recall the first French invasion of Portugal in 1807 which aimed to seize the 'blue water' Portuguese fleet after the Franco-Spanish defeat of Trafalgar in 1805. However, the Portuguese navy not completely immobilized during this period. Indeed, it was committed to two relatively important campaigns, even though between the first (Cayenne conquest of 1809) and second (occupation of eastern band, 1816-17) an interval of seven years had elapsed.

The damage resulting from the war with France was relatively minor for the warships concerned, and between 1809 and 1814 only 1 frigate and 3 brigs were lost to enemy action. Moreover, the squadron underwent a considerable increase in numbers during this period – a ship of the line, 5 frigates, 3 corvettes, 8 brigs and 3 schooners. Of these, 3 frigates, 2 corvettes, 7 brigs and 3 schooners, approximately 45 percent of the total, were constructed in Brazilian naval arsenals. Moreover, the government purchased or armed 2 frigates, 11 corvettes, 6 brigs, 6 transports and 2 schooners, one-fifth of which (including ships of the line) were increased to reinforce the occupation of the Eastern Band or Uruguai (1816-17).

Brazil having proclaimed its independence, most of the Portuguese warship crews stationed there joined D. Pedro's cause, with mutinies in Rio de Janeiro and Montevideo. Thus, 8 ships of the line, 4 frigates, 6 corvettes, 6 brigs, 14 schooners and 3 smaller ships were transferred to the Brazilian authorities. The once powerful Portuguese Navy was now reduced by 65 percent. The impact of this, when considering the economic and strategic loss of Brazil, had a major impact during the subsequent Miguelite Wars of 1828 to 1834. In 1831 the almost unopposed seizure of minor Portuguese warships on the Tagus river by the French naval squadrons of Rabaudy and Roussin lead to the loss of 3 frigates, 3 corvettes, 3 brigs and 1 transport, which were 25 percent of Miguelite naval strength.

Miguelite fleet (Various commanders)

Third Rate Ship of the Line *Rainha* with 74 guns.
Third Rate Ship of the Line *D. João* with 74 guns.
Fourth Rate Ship of the Line *Martinho de Freitas* with 50 guns.
Fifth Rate Heavy Frigate *Duquesa da Bragança* with an exceptional garrison of 56 guns (probably overrated with carronades).
Sixth Rate Frigate (classified in the Portuguese Navy as Corvette) *Isabel Maria* with 22 guns.
Sixth Rate Frigate (rated in the Portuguese Navy as Corvette) *Princesa Real* with 24 guns.
Sixth Rate Frigate (classified in the Portuguese Navy as Corvette) *Tejo* with 20 guns.

Sixth Rate Frigate (classified in the Portuguese Navy as Corvette) *Sybille* with 20 guns.
Unrated Brig *Audaz* with 18 guns.
Unrated Xebec *Activa*, probably 12 guns.
Several other brigs and xebecs armed with 3 to 6 guns

Navy Royal Brigade

The Naval Royal Brigade was established by a Regulation of 28 August 1797. This maritime corps was the heir to sections of armed fleet sailors known as *Terços Reais de Marinha*. Its mission was to serve as naval infantry for landings and field operations; ship defence or boarding assault. The brigade was also ensure to the safety of ground installations such as naval arsenals and fortresses and, if necessary, to provide gun crews for ships and on land. Moreover, it provided shipboard marines and ballast craftsmen (the latter category being rare). Between one third and one fifth of ship crews were members of this corps. In 1822, the Navy Royal Brigade had 925 men, including 98 officers (4 generals), 200 sergeants, corporals and drums, and 627 soldiers. In 1828, the corps was expanded to 1,278 men. In Lisbon, on 22 December 1828, a brigade revolt in support of the Liberal cause was planned, but postponed to 9 January 1829. The major conspirators were the brigadier and former brigade commander Alexandre José Moreira Freire along with other junior officers. The revolt failed and the conspirators executed for treason. The brigade officers were replaced with those loyal, but not necessarily as competent as their predecessors, to D. Miguel. Following the failed coup, the Miguelite marines were dispersed throughout the fleet and in the Lisbon fortress defending the Tagus.

On 8 July 1833, following the defeat of the Miguelite Navy at the Battle of St. Vincent, the Duke of Terceira recruited men of the fo Navy Royal Brigade into the Liberal army. The reconstituted brigade was composed of well-equipped and well-disciplined veterans who landed in Lagos and were part of the Duke of Terceira's operations to capture Lisbon.

Navy Royal Brigade Uniforms (Plate 22)

Sailor Gunners – Gunners uniforms of the newly created Navy Royal Brigade were also regulated and evolved until the civil war. The parade uniform consisted of a short blue coat with bands (lapels) of the same colour. The piping, collar and cuffs were of red cloth and the buttons were yellow with an engraved anchor. On the left sleeve, above the cuff, they wore a 'Naval Gun' patch in yellow cloth. Pantaloons were white, long, and had a flap covering the shoe straps rather than having a gaiter feature. The shakos were of black leather (for harsh sea conditions), with a red wool tuft, the letters 'AM' (Navy Gunners), intertwined in yellow metal. Their armament was a short sword with yellow metal cups and a flintlock pistol attached to a cross belt of the sword. The shipboard uniform was a sleeveless vest, of blue cloth, with red-necked collars, long denim pants and flat shoes without laces.

Later, a new legislation changed the band colours to red. The uniform was now a blue cloth jacket, with red bands and cuffs and a red collar. A white cloth vest and blue cloth shorts were the service dress for winter, and long cloth shorts and a linen or denim vest for summer. The wearing of a black tie, a pair of gaiters, and a black leather shako were regulated. The buttons remained yellow with an anchor.

Sergeants of Sailor Gunners – For sergeants, the uniforms were the same as those of gunners, but were distinguished by epaulettes. They also wore the artillery gun in yellow metal on the sleeve, the shako had red feathers and the letters AM in yellow metal, intertwined and covered by a metal Royal Crown. Their winter uniform was blue pantaloons with black cloth gaiters. Rank distinctions are made as follows:

Sergeants – Two blue cloth epaulettes trimmed with gold fringe.
Junior Sergeants – One blue cloth epaulette trimmed with gold fringe on the right shoulder.
Corporals – One blue cloth epaulette trimmed with gold fringe on the left shoulder.

Sailor Artillery Officers

The officers wore the same uniform as the Navy Royal Brigade, distinguishing themselves by wearing a gold embroidered artillery gun patch on the left sleeve above the cuff cannon. Red feathers were worn on shakos. On guard, parade, exercise, or other services, officers sported a band and collar in accordance with the model determined by the Navy Inspector General. Artillery gun patches were sewn on all uniforms. In the winter, they wore boots with blue pantaloons and on duty they wore long trousers. On duty and as a matter of routine, they wore a metal neck collar, probably of yellow metal, and a band (tassel-wrapped cloth) that distinguished all officers.

Marines – The established Marine Corps, from its origin on 28 August 1797, was the same as that of the Naval Gunners: a short blue jacket with blue lapels, red collar lining and cuffs, and yellow buttons with anchor. The vest was white together with the long, short-fitting, white pantaloons. The Marines also wore a black leather shako with red lace and a red feather on the left. For barracks uniform, they wore blue sleeveless vests with red collars and long denim pantaloons. They distinguished themselves by not wearing the artillery gun patch on their left sleeve and by having the interwoven letters FM (Marine Fusiliers) on issue leather shakos. Their armament consisted of a flintlock musket, of Portuguese or British manufacture and bayonet. Later than 1806, the uniform was red piped, and above the left cuff they started to sport a gold-embroidered musket. The white summer vest was made of denim or linen and the one worn in the winter was made in white cloth. The regulation also foresaw the use of a black tie and gaiters with buttons.

By 1826, Marine uniforms were of the French style with white pantaloons, white sword lanyards, open blue jackets with red bands and a large bell-topped shako with a big red plume, maintaining all earlier issue garments, accouterments and armaments.

Battle of Cape St. Vincent

The Miguelite government reacted strongly when they heard of the unexpected Liberal naval expedition dispatched in early summer 1833. Its mission was to disembark 2,500 men in the Algarve before marching to Lisbon through the Alentejo from there. In late June 1833, the Miguelite navy began to chase after the Liberal fleet (already under the command of Admiral Charles Napier) sending their main squadron under the command of Admiral Antonio Torres de Aboim. The Miguelite fleet was a great force, consisting of 2 ships of line, 2 frigates, 3 corvettes, and 2 brigs. The opposing squadrons met on 3 July, but only after two days of manoeuvring on the morning of the 5 July did the fighting take place off Cape St. Vincent. Hesitation at the beginning of the fight was unfavourable to the Miguelite squadron, since in the meantime there had been a calmness of wind and sea that allowed the Liberal squadron to make a bold move and launch an attack against the approaching enemy ships of the line. By resorting to close combat, avoiding the traditional artillery clash with in-line manoeuvres, Napier was able to nullify the numerical and firepower advantage of the Miguelite naval forces. The commander of the Miguelite squadron, adhering to the conventional naval combat tactics dominated by the Portuguese naval officers, was surprised by Napier's audacity and tactical flexibility. This combat, which could be considered a battle between the British and the Portuguese, since not only the admiral of the Liberal squadron but the commanders of the main force ships were British, resulted in the seizure of ships, frigates and a corvette of the Miguelite squadron. This was a defeat of tremendous proportions Only the Miguelite corvette *Isabel Maria* and the corvette *Cibele* were able to escape to Lisbon. Brig *Tejo* sought refuge on the island of Madeira and Brig *Audaz* surrendered in Lagos the following day. With this battle, the armada loyal to D. Miguel practically disappeared, leaving the Liberals with the full dominion of the sea. The Liberal Navy grew immensely with the capture of the Miguelite ships. This sea battle was, in addition to being a remarkable tactical achievement, a decisive strategic victory.

Battle of Cape St. Vincent, 5 July 1833 by Morel-Fatio. (National Library of Portugal)

Liberal fleet at St. Vincent (Charles Napier)

- Fifth Rate Great Frigate *Rainha de Portugal* with 46 guns, as flagship, under the command of Commodore Wilkinson and Captain MacDonough
- Fifth Rate Great Frigate *Dona Maria* with 42 guns, under the command of Captain Peake
- Fifth Rate Great Frigate *D. Pedro* with 50 guns, under the command of Captain Thomas Goble. This frigate was added to the squadron during the Siege of Porto and was not present at the landing of D. Pedro's Army, 8 July 1832.
- Unrated Corvette *Vila Flor* with 18 guns, under the command of Acting Captain Ruxton.
- Unrated Brig *Portuense* with 20 guns under the command of Acting Captain Blackstone.
- Unrated Schooner *Faro* with 6 guns
- A small force of steam tugs and transports

Miguelite fleet at St. Vincent (Admiral António Torres de Aboim)

- Third Rate Ship of the Line *Rainha* with 74 guns, under the command of Captain Barradas and captured by the Liberal heavy frigate *Rainha de Portugal.*
- Third Rate Ship of the Line *D. João* with 74 guns, captured by the Liberal squadron.
- Fourth Rate Ship of the Line *Martinho de Freitas* with 50 guns, captured by the Liberal squadron
- Fifth Rate Heavy Frigate *Duquesa da Bragança* with an exceptional garrison of 56 guns (probably overrated due to the use of carronades), captured by the Liberal heavy frigate *Dona Maria*.
- Sixth Rate Frigate (classified in the Portuguese Navy as corvette) *Isabel Maria* with 22 guns, captured by the Liberal squadron.
- Sixth Rate Frigate (rated in the Portuguese Navy as corvette) *Princesa Real* with 24 guns, captured by the Liberal squadron.
- Sixth Rate Frigate (classified in the Portuguese Navy as corvette) *Tejo* with 20 guns, managed to escape.
- Sixth Rate Frigate (classified in the Portuguese Navy as corvette) *Sybille* with 20 guns, managed to escape.
- Unrated Brig *Audaz* with 18 guns, managed to escape.
- Unrated Xebec *Activa*, probably 12 guns, managed to escape.
- Several other unnamed brigs also fled to Lisbon and Madeira.

Sketch of Napier's glorious triumph over the Miguelite squadron by George Philip Reinagle, 1833. (National Library of Portugal)

Battle of Cape Saint Vincent 1833. (*Clark's Battles and Tales*)

Part II

The War of the Two Brothers Timeline of a Civil War

Revolution of 24 August 1820 and Path to War

Europe, 26 September 1815: Formation of the Holy Alliance. In 1815, the absolutist and conservative national powers of Austria, Prussia and Russia formed the Holy Alliance to counter, often in a violent way, the emerging Liberal movements in Europe, especially in Belgium, Southern Europe and Italy.

Portugal, 1816: When Queen Maria I of Portugal, emerged in a serious mental disorder since the bloody fate of their cousins Louis XVI and Marie Antoinette during the French Revolution, died in March 1816, her son, the Prince Regent, effective ruler since 1806, was crowned King D. João VI of Portugal and Brazil. King João VI and his Spanish wife Queen Carlota-Joaquina, the sister of Ferdinand VII of Spain, had two sons and three daughters. Their sons would become enemies and the banners of two opposing views on ruling. These two would plunge the country into a harsh and bloody civil war; the first-born D. Pedro, a paladin of moderate Liberalism, on one side, and D. Miguel, a radical absolutist, on the other.

Queen Maria I. (National Library of Portugal)

Iberian Peninsula, 1820: The Liberal uprisings in Spain and Portugal: In the early months of 1820, a Liberal uprising broke out amongst Spanish troops stationed at the city and harbour of Cadiz. This military mutiny forced King

Ferdinand VII of Spain to declare himself in favour of a constitutional regime, although for a brief time, and paving the way for three civil wars during the 19th century, known generally as the Carlist Wars.

In Portugal, the effective commander of the Portuguese Army and ruler of the country itself, the well-known British Marshal William Carr Beresford, responsible for the rebirth of the Portuguese Army of the Peninsular Wars, sailed to Brazil in an attempt to persuade King João VI to give him more ruling powers.

Coup of 24 August 1820: During the absence of King D. João VI at the Rio de Janeiro Court, on the 24 of August 1820, a secret proto-masonic society named *Sinedrio*, mainly formed from magistrates, lawyers, tradesmen, and businessmen, with the support of Army officers, triggered an uprising in Porto. Not all of them Liberals, but all were against British rule over the Portuguese Army that had been in place since the Peninsular War. The movement spread and quickly took over the government of Portugal. In October 1820, Marshal Beresford, returning from Brazil, tried to land in Portugal but he was denied permission and sailed back to England.

Portugal, July 1821: In July 1821, King D. João VI arrived in Portugal, leaving his son, Prince D. Pedro of Bragança, to rule in Brazil, although already aware that the path to Brazilian independence would, headed by D. Pedro, commence shortly afterwards.

Manuel Fernandes Thomaz, one of the leaders of *Sinedrio* secret association and the Liberal coup of 24 August 1820. (National Library of Portugal)

Brazil, 7 September 1822: Proclamation of Brazilian independence by Prince D. Pedro of Alcantara. He became Emperor Pedro I of Brazil, following the path of the South American movements of self-determination. However, it was a unique monarchy in that it was a fully organized state, economically and politically stable and with an army and navy. Thus, history would show that Brazil would become the primay power in South America.

Portugal, 23 September 1822: First Portuguese constitution established. The result was a Portuguese government dominated by Liberal and radical Constitutionalists. King D. João VI had no choice other than to approve Portugal's first Constitution. His wife, Queen Carlota-Joaquina, refused to swear to the Constitution and was sent into exile. She would become the leader of the counterrevolutionaries and gain the support of her younger son, Prince D. Miguel.

12 October 1822: D. João VI's son D. Pedro I was acclaimed as constitutional emperor of Brazil on 12 October 1822. King João VI retained the sovereignty of Portugal, but the real victor was Queen Carlota-Joaquina, whose counter-revolutionary conspiracies gained strength; the King's power waned and paved the way for a future civil war.

First Absolutist Reactions Against the Liberals

27 May 1823: The Vilafrancada Movement: The absolutists in Portugal saw their chance and, on 27 May 1823, quickly raised a rebellion. The Count of Amarante, a leading absolutist and warlord, sounded a call for an uprising from his headquarters at Vila Real in Trás-os-Montes (northwestern Portugal). Meanwhile, the military absolutist ranks rose at Vila Franca de Xira, north of Lisbon, hence the name of the episode, the Vilafrancada. King D. João's younger son, D. Miguel, quickly joined the rebellion, as did many regiments of the Lisbon garrison. D. Miguel refused his father's orders to push back, and subsequently, King D. João VI took responsibility for containment of the rebellion. The Liberal radical government fell apart and King D. João gave way to moderate rule, but this was to be a failed attempt to prevent a political and military crisis.

The Vilafrancada Absolutist coup led by D. Miguel. (National Library of Portugal)

April 1824: The Abrilada Coup: In April 1824, part of the Lisbon garrison again acclaimed D. Miguel as absolute king in a true coup d'état. Prince D. Miguel once again promptly joined them and this time imprisoned his father in the royal palace. Some of his enemies were also arrested or driven into exile.

Marshal Beresford managed to get King João aboard a British warship, from where he reasserted his power and had D. Miguel stripped of his rank (*Generalíssimo dos Exércitos* or Master General of the Armies) sending him abroad to exile, first to Paris and then Vienna. The Abrilada coup, as it would become known, lasted for only five days. Although some politicians asked for stronger British military presence in Portugal, they only kept a naval squadron, including a reinforced battalion of 750 Royal Marines, in Lisbon.

29 August 1825: Brazilian Independence: On 29 August 1825, the independence of the Brazilian Empire was recognized with a treaty; King D. João VI and his older son, D. Pedro I, Emperor of Brazil, finally and officially cut colonial ties between Brazil and Portugal. Brazil would become a strong military power in South America.

10 March 1826: King João VI of Portugal died on 10 March 1826. His eldest son, Pedro I of Brazil, briefly inherited the kingdom as Pedro IV of Portugal, but this situation would not be sustainable since Pedro could not inherit two Crowns. Portugal was in a serious succession crisis, with the growing abyss between the Liberal and Absolutist parties.

29 April 1826: Neither the Portuguese nor the Brazilians want a unified monarchy, and D. Pedro de Bragança abdicated the Portuguese throne in favour of his seven-year-old daughter, Dona Maria da Glória of Portugal. There was a key condition: when she came of age (14 years), she would marry her uncle, D. Miguel, still in his Vienna exile. The announcement conveniently coincided with a revision to the radical 1822 constitution which reinforced the King's powers. D. Pedro then returned to Brazil with his daughter, the future Queen of Portugal, leaving his sister Dona Maria Isabel as regent.

First Shots of the Civil War

22 February 1828: On 22 February 1828, D. Miguel returned to Portugal, and on 26 February, he took the oath to his brother, D. Pedro, and to the 1826 Constitutional Chart and was installed as lieutenant-general for the king. His loyalty did not last long (if it ever existed), and it was an act of political deception from D. Miguel who wanted to get closer to power.

March 1828: D. Miguel I and his mother, former Queen Carlota-Joaquina, after suppressing the Constitutional Chart, immediately began to pursue the Liberals, both the radicals and the moderates and installing their trusty followers, many of them rogue absolutists from all social levels. D. Miguel quickly dissolved the Chamber of Deputies and the Chamber of Peers. All demonstrations in favour of D. Pedro or the constitution were prohibited as acts of treason, which could mean exile, prison, or death by hanging.

24 April 1828: The British troops in Lisbon and the naval squadron were withdrawn as a feeble protest against D. Miguel's usurpation but without any real effects on the Miguelite regime.

16 May 1828: This event was known as the *Belfastada*. A group of exiled Liberals landed in Porto after disembarking form the English ship *Belfast* and raised a rebellion. The rebellion failed and the senior Liberals were forced to take refuge back aboard the *Belfast* and leave again for England. On the 16 May 1828, the garrison of Porto proclaimed its support for D. Pedro, Dona Maria da Glória, and the Constitutional Chart. The 12th Caçadores Battalion, with Major Silva Pereira, was part of the garrison and was one the most active units of the uprising. The city of Aveiro, the south of Porto, and other places soon followed Porto's lead. D. Miguel brutally suppressed these rebellions; many thousands of Liberals were either arrested or fled to Spain and Britain. Twelve Liberals were arrested, submitted to a special court, the Alçada, sentenced to be hanged, their bodies beheaded, and the heads put on stakes through northern Portugal. They were executed in May of 1829 and since then they've been known as the Martyrs of Liberty. Five years of harsh repression followed. Of all Portuguese territory, only the Azores islands remained loyal to D. Pedro, particularly Terceira Island, partly because the garrison stayed faithful, especially the 5th Caçadores Battalion.

15 June 1828: Having declared for D. Pedro in May, Major Silva Pereira and the 12 Caçadores Battalion engaged in guerrilla warfare and defeated a Miguelite column at the Espinhel bridge on 15 June 1828. Silva Pereira subsequently went to England, where he joined other Portuguese exiles.

8 July 1828: One of the most important supporters of D. Pedro, the Count of Vila Flor arrived in Village of the Beach (Vila da Praia) on the island of Terceira in the Azores, having sailed from France and avoided the Miguelite navy blockade. He began to fortify the island.

11 July 1828: On 11 July 1828, D. Miguel was proclaimed king by the traditional Royal Court. The United States and Mexico were the only two countries to recognize him; in contrast, the Holy Alliance, Great Britain, Austria, France, Naples and Spain protested the illegal suppression of the constitution.

Kiss D. Pédro! by Daumier. (National Library of Portugal)

The Azores goes Liberal

11 August 1829: D. Miguel sent a squadron of 22 warships to the Azores, which were mostly controlled by D. Pedro and his troops. The Miguelite squadron attacked the fortifications in the bay near the Village of the Beach (Vila da Praia), on the island of Terceira. After a day of battle, the Liberals under the Count of Vila Flor emerged victorious with hundreds of prisoners. After the war, the village was renamed Victory Beach (Praia da Vitória) to commemorate the battle. The first sliver of light in the absolutist darkness came in the Azores. D. Miguel had ordered a purge of the Portuguese army and navy, sacking all supposed Liberal officers – as the army in particular was regarded as containing many Liberal sympathizers, some 60 percent of the officer corps was purged. This did nothing for the efficiency of either the Portuguese army or the navy, as events were to show, and many of the ablest Portuguese officers were sacked. They scattered across Europe and Brazil, and one, General Torres, born in 1782, a veteran of the Peninsular War, was a solid, reliable and efficient officer, landed in the Island of Terceira. Defeating the numerous local forces loyal to D. Miguel with a small force of volunteer artillerymen and a detachment of the 5th Caçadores battalion, he seized the island for Dona Maria. The exiles made their way there, the Count de Vila Flor taking full command. At Vila da Praia, a Miguelite fleet from Portugal tried to land 6,000 soldiers to retake the island. The first detachment was defeated on landing; then a second was also defeated and the fleet sailed away. In 1831, Vila Flor lead a force to capture the nearby island of S. Jorge and the other islands followed, the last of which, S. Miguel, falling to a force of 1,400 men under Vila Flor, which landed and routed a force of 5,000 troops equipped with plenty of artillery. The weaknesses of the Portuguese Army were becoming apparent – the officers were poor, the men, once beaten, rapidly changed sides and the Liberal force accordingly grew, although its overall reliability was somewhat questionable.

The Liberal Victory in the Azores. The Battle of Praia da Vitória. (Engraving courtesy of Queluz National Palace Archives)

20 January 1830: Following this victory, the Count of Vila Flor proceeded to secure the remainder of the archipelago. With 1,400 men, including the 5th Caçadores, and a few vessels, he took the islands of Pico, S. Jorge, Faial, and S. Miguel. He was outnumbered; S. Miguel alone had more than Miguelite 3,000 defenders, but the Liberal troops managed to land and secure the victory.

July 1830: The French Bourbons were replaced by Liberal monarchy of Louis-Philippe. The new government began to favour the exiled Spanish Liberals. About this time, the French sent a naval squadron to the Tagus. Admiral Roussin fired on the batteries at the mouth of the Tagus, with a very weak and feeble resistance from the river fortresses, seizing two Portuguese warships and rescuing a group of French citizens threatened by the Miguelite government.

April 1831: Emperor Pedro I abdicated in Brazil in favour of his son, Pedro II, and sailed for Britain where he began to organise a military expedition, which would be completed in France, at Belle-Isle, in the Atlantic shores.

February 1832: The Liberal expedition sailed for the Azores, which were already in the hands of the Liberals.

March 1832: D. Pedro set up an exile government in Terceira Island. The city of Angra became the capital of the Constitutional Kingdom of Portugal.

27 June 1832: At the end of June 1832, D. Pedro's fleet sailed from the Azores. He took with him 8,300 men, 2 frigates, a corvette, 2 brigs, 4 schooners, 40 sail transports, and 3 guns of light field artillery. D. Pedro left behind detachments on S. Miguel and Terceira islands. The Terceira detachment was ordered to create a National Battalion (presumably volunteer units), which became the 4th Line Infantry (disbanded in 1830 by D. Miguel after several uprisings and creating a new unit called the New Infantry Regiment of Lisbon) and served in the lines of Porto and Lisbon and the subsequent campaign.

Siege of Porto

8 July 1832: Pedro's Liberal army landed at the beaches between Mindelo and Arnosa de Pampelido, the northern shores of Porto, taking the inner routes to Porto through the Maia lands to avoid the seaside roads due to the danger of being intercepted by the Miguelite Navy. They arrived at the City of Porto the following day (9 July), entering through the Carvalhido streets in the northern outskirts of the city. The Liberal columns did not find any resistance from the Miguelite garrison, which retreated to the south side of the River Douro, but quickly started to encircle Porto to enclose the Liberal army inside the city and avoid their possible retreat back to the naval squadron.

Commencement of the Siege of Porto (Cerco do Porto), 9 July 1832-20 August 1833: D.Pedro, Duke of Bragança, former Emperor of Brazil and then King of Portugal, entered Porto with his 8,300 man multi-national army on 9 July 1832 and was immediately besieged by the Miguelite forces of the Porto garrison, about 18,000 men strong, to be later reinforced until it reached over 30,000 men, mostly regular troops, but also with thousands of men of the Royalist Volunteers and numerous irregular bands.

Unaware of the number of the approaching Liberals, the 13,000 Miguelite defenders of Porto abandoned the city. The Miguelite General Santa Marta, commander of the Miguelite garrison of Northern Portugal, operating between the Figueira da Foz and the village of Vila do Conde, decided to deploy his infantry

Landing of the liberal forces in Oporto on 8 July 1832 by Johann Michael Voltz 1784-1858. (Author's collection)

brigades, cavalry, and field artillery in the village of Vila Nova de Gaia, and sent some regiments north around the outskirts of Porto to check the Liberals' advance to the city. The Liberal army entered Porto unopposed, although Santa Marta's men began to fire into the city with field guns, but without any significant damage. To defend the south, the Liberal troops posted a 600 men garrison in the Serra Convent. The Serra of Pilar is a range of hills located near Santa Marinha (Vila Nova de Gaia) on the south bank of the River Douro. It had the only Liberal redoubt (a convent) south of the river which it controlled, thus allowing the defenders to land essential provisions. Lovell Badcock, who visited the Serra redoubt during the siege, on the 12 January 1833, considered that it had weak defences and a large perimeter to be defended by only a battalion of 600 to 700 men. Consequently, Lovell admired the commander and his men for managing to defend it. The key to the city itself was the Serra of Pilar on a cliff across the river. If the Miguelites took the position, any batteries erected there could destroy the city with ease. Occupied for a short time at the very beginning of the siege by the Miguelites, it was seized in September 1832 and fortified by the Liberals, reportedly on the insistence of Colonel Hare, a supposedly neutral observer sent by the British Government. Fortified as strongly as possible, it withstood constant bombardment and heavy assault throughout the siege. In command was the veteran Torres, usually referred to by the British as 'old Torres', who lived in a shed built against the walls. He inspired his garrison in their desperate defence, the men being made up of a few regulars, large numbers of volunteers and 'movable' and 'fixed' militia. The defenders inflicted heavy casualties on the attackers and were reported as having supplied their cannons with solid shots fired at them.

To protect British interests, a naval squadron under Commander William Glascock (commanding HMS *Orestes* frigate and 2 brigs was stationed in the Douro, where it came under fire from both sides. There it remained in what was ultimately a neutral place in the river ready to evacuate Porto's British colony most of which were wine merchants.

10 July 1832: The Liberal admiral, George Sartorius, with 16 fighting ships, among them 2 heavy frigates of 46 and 42 guns, ordered the lighter warships to enter the bar of the River Douro and to respond to the Miguelite batteries with light artillery fire. Meanwhile, protected by the brigs from the Sartorius naval squadron, the Liberal light division formed by the Caçadores battalions 2, 3 and 5, under the command of the irascible German-born Lieutenant Colonel Joahnn Schwalbach, crossed the river and occupied the Serra of Pilar, the old monastery in Gaia, later fortified, compelling the Miguelite forces to withdraw to the towns of Grijó and Oliveira de Azeméis. Schwalbach light troops then advanced to the heights of Alto da Bandeira (literally Height of the Flag, nowadays still holding the memory of the place) and positioned his advance guard in the nearby village of Carvalhos. This brought the two armies into close contact, at musket fire range, staring and waiting. Neither side, except for some infantry advances and light skirmishing, wanted to escalate the action at that time.

14-18 July 1832: The Liberals in Porto, still in small numbers and without clear support from the population, repulsed the first Miguelite attacks, weak and poorly managed, since there were no barricades or batteries at the time. Most of the combat was at bayonet point at the cover of farms walls, and only the resilience of the Liberal troops managed to hold the positions. Also, the poorly led Miguelite soldiers had the habit to break up the attack columns and open in lines, which was ineffective against defensive lines. In the weeks after taking positions in Porto, D. Pedro had 8,544 soldiers plus 2,100 city volunteers and conscripts, still a risky situation facing the increasing numbers of Miguelite troops taking positions around the city. Although the Liberals retained the Serra of Pilar fortifications on the south bank of the river, they had had to abandon the three major heights to the north (Regado, Antas, and Covelo), and hardly retaining the position of Lordelo that linked the city with the estuary of the River Douro. Despite the lack of good officers, it did not take much to realise that by cutting the route between Foz and Porto, the city could be easily starved into surrender. Vanzeller Farm, a country villa and walled garden belonging to one of the great English wine shipping families, became a well-defended strongpoint but the only other batteries and entrenchments lay round the hamlet of Lordelo and they were small and relatively weak. Six-hundred Scots had arrived from the slums of Edinburgh and Glasgow in late 1832 and a considerable group of rogues was put under the command of Captain Charles Shaw, promoted to Major, and given the task to train and lead the future Scottish Battalion. He used rather unorthodox methods, shaming the recalcitrant, rather than using the traditional flogging, by blackening their noses, removing the tartan from their forage caps or other imaginative ways to shame a Scotsman by another Scotsman. He tried hard to stop them drinking too, but in this harsh task he had some help. In February 1833, he was ordered to take his Scottish Fusiliers, as they were now termed, to Lordelo for three days. They stayed for six months and came under the heaviest attacks mounted against the Porto defences. On several occasions his men sustained heavy casualties whilst giving an excellent account of themselves. Shaw had particularly trained them in the use of the bayonet and the Miguelites came to fear the terrifying charges of these wild, half-starved Scotsmen urged on by shrieking bagpipes since Shaw even had three pipers.

Other British troops sent to this sector included a battalion of Irish raised and led by Colonel Cotter and his son. They also took heavy casualties in the desperate defence in July 1833, and both Cotter and his son were killed. A recently arrived English battalion was also sent there under Colonel Dodgin. These men would become the core of the English Grenadier Battalion or Regiment.

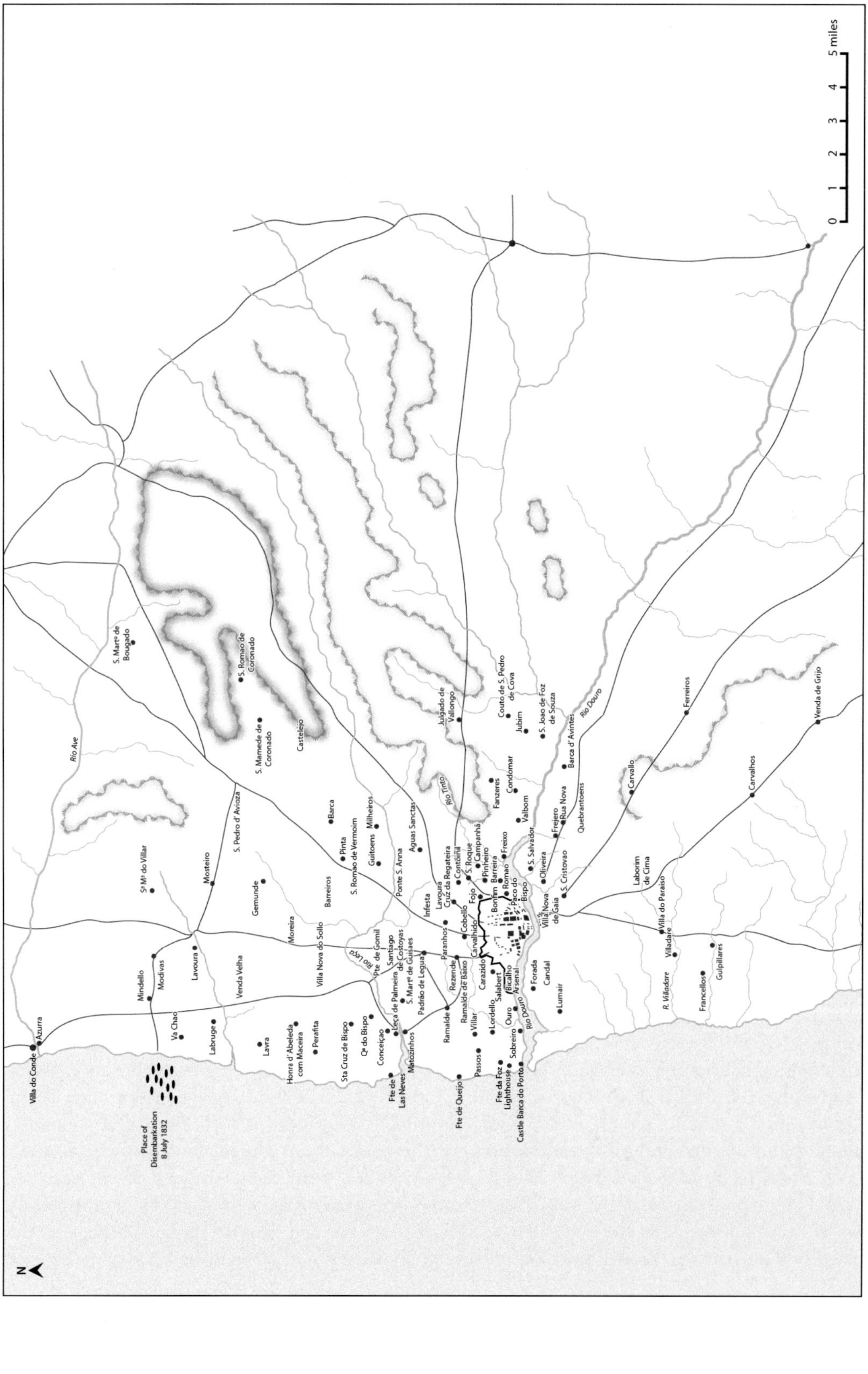

Liberal Army landing and assaults, 1832.

18 July 1832: The Liberal Command ordered a sortie at Penafiel, always towards north. A Liberal column forced a passage through the Miguelite forces around Porto, attacked the city of Penafiel, and then returned to Porto, due to dearth of numbers. The iron ring was closing around the Liberals. The Miguelite command, headed by the Generals Viscount of Santa Marta and General Álvaro Xavier da Fonseca Coutinho e Póvoas met at Souto Redondo, to the south of the Douro, encircled Porto with four divisions and a mobile, brigade-sized column. Eventually, there were approximately 30,000 Miguelite troops surrounding the city.

22 July 1832: Still wanting to test the enemy capacity to react and mobilize, D. Pedro ordered a column to make a reconnaissance towards the northern village of Valongo near Porto. The 5th Caçadores Battalion, including Major Silva Pereira, were part of this force together with regular infantry units. Again this was an inconclusive operation after an exchange of heavy musketry fire, and again the Liberals had to return to Porto. This operation demonstrated to D. Pedro and his generals that they were surrounded by far superior Miguelite forces thus, confirming news of the arrival of some 20,000 reinforcements for Santa Marta and Álvaro Xavier da Fonseca Coutinho e Póvoas. The future of their besieged force uncertain, D. Pedro's headquarters began to consider a withdrawal back to Azores.

23 July 1832: Despite the growing menace of the Miguelite forces, the Liberal command once again sent a heavy column north for Valongo. it fell into a Miguelite ambush near the bridge known as Ponte de Ferreira and was forced to withdraw to the River Tinto with heavy loss, hardly managing to halt the retreat of panic-stricken troops. The Battle of Ponte Ferreira caused alarm in the northern environs of Porto and, as a precaution, the Liberals reinforced the south front, and Serra of Pilar was fortified under Major Sá Nogueira. D. Pedro, who now recognized the impossibility of occupying northern Portugal, settled into Porto and prepared to resist a siege that was already a certainty. Reorganizing his forces, D. Pedro formed a general staff. He also sent Pedro de Sousa Holstein to London to obtain financial support and raise more men, primarily foreigners: Belgians, Italians, French, Germans and more British mercenaries.

27 July 1832: A violent combat took place to the south of Grijó, near Vila Nova de Gaia. The Miguelite General Álvaro Xavier da Fonseca Coutinho e Póvoas once again defeated the Liberal forces of the Count of Vila Flor, who tried a reconnaissance attack without the capacity of holding ground and had to retreat with his troops to Alto da Bandeira. Their retreat was supported by the Liberal 10th Infantry Regiment led by Bernardo de Sá Nogueira, who was severely wounded in his right arm by a musket ball above the elbow, later to be amputated.

During these actions, the Miguelite command made changes at the operational headquarters due to the constant quarrels between their two main generals, Álvaro Xavier da Fonseca Coutinho e Póvoas and Santa Marta. A former supporter of the Liberal movement of 24 August 1820, General Gaspar Teixeira de Lacerda, Viscount of Peso da Régua, now a harsh enemy of the Liberals, was appointed the supreme Miguelite commander over Generals Álvaro Xavier da Fonseca Coutinho e Póvoas and Santa Marta. Soon, and with a remarkable speed, Gaspar Teixeira started building extended siege lines around Porto. These consisted of a series of strong redoubts with an initial deployment of 15 heavy artillery batteries including 24 and 36 pounders guns and mortars. In the north, these batteries bombarded the whole valley of Campanhã up to the still fragile Liberal defensive lines, these being built at a slower rate than their Miguelite opponents. At the Douro River bar, the Miguelite artillery fired solid shot and bombs against the Liberal ramparts of the huge fortress of S. João da Foz and Senhora da Luz barricades, and threatened ship movements through the Douro Estuary. To the south, the Miguelite heavy guns covered

Battle of Ponte Ferreira 23 July 1832 by A. E. Hoffman (18??-18??), a foreign officer who fought under Pedro, Duke of Braganza's. (National Palace of Queluz)

the Cabedelo sand track, which partly enclosed the Douro Estuary, and up the river they could range their fire until the river beaches of Pedra Salgada on the southern banks of the Douro, facing the heights of the Seminary, in the northern bank where the Liberals would build one of the most powerful batteries, including 24 pounder guns. This allowed them to cover the isolated Liberal positions of Serra of Pilar.

7 August 1832: The Miguelites again defeated weak Liberal forces at Souto Redondo, forcing them to withdraw with heavy casualties. These sorties were mainly reconnaissance in force movements to identify the menace of hostile division reinforcements. However, with limited numbers and a growing casualty list, it soon became apparent at Liberal Headquarters that Porto had to be rapidly fortified with extensive lines of trenches, palisades and covered tracks connecting the small forts and redoubts situated about the 12 km perimeter.

8 August 1832: In the meantime, the Miguelite forces started their own offensive movements, mostly reconnaissance sorties to harass the Liberal defences in the northern part of Porto. The Miguelite infantry and Caçadores brigades were stationed in large encampments 4 km away from the outer lines of the Liberal forces, facing the S. Mamede Infesta village and the surrounding plains, mostly farms and pastures. These small scale attacks had the purpose of providing a true understanding of the Liberal capacity of holding their lines, but again the tactical approach of the Miguelites was advancing in close columns, quite in

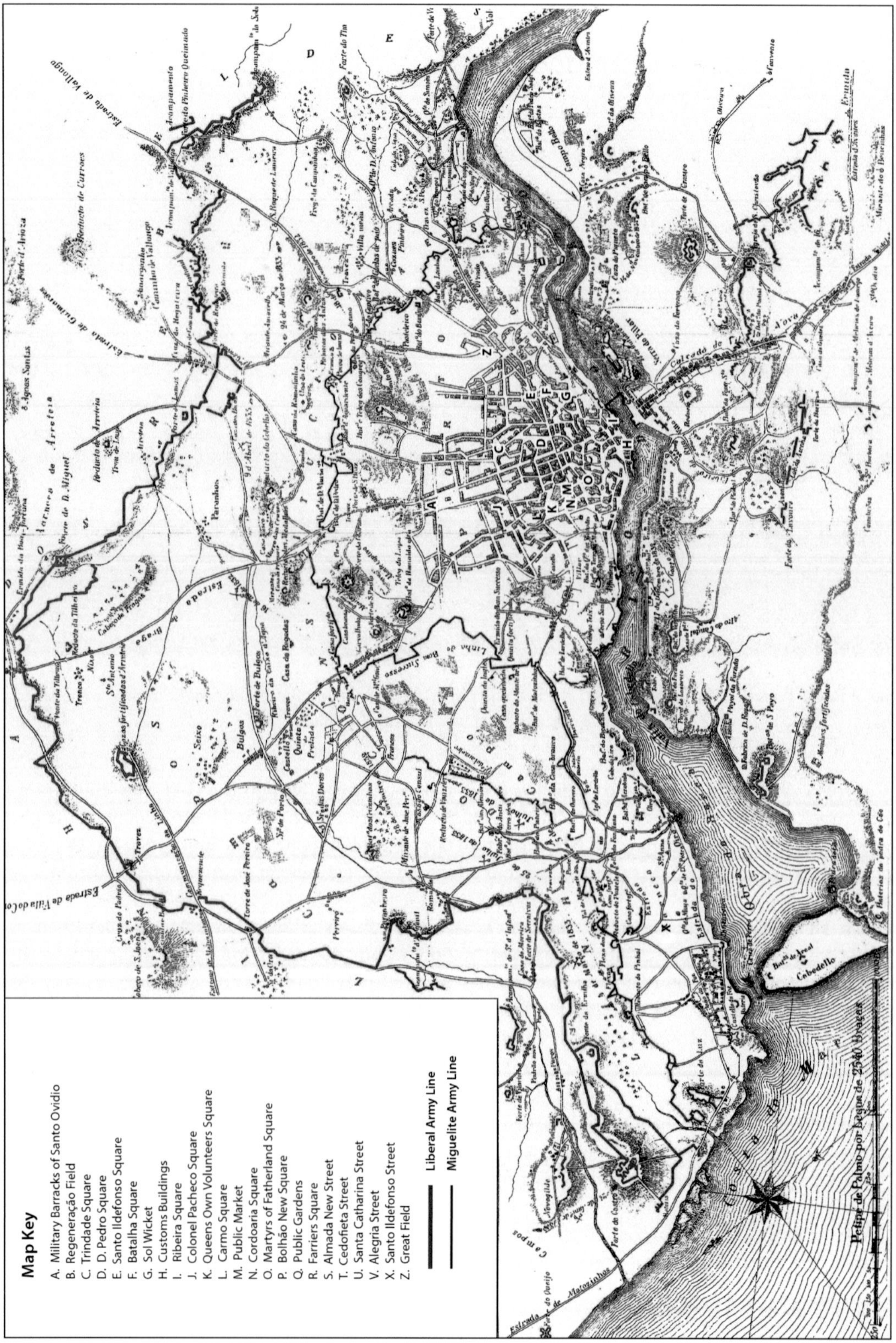

Map of Siege of Porto based on map by Royal Engineer Colonel Moreira, 1833.

the French style, but again the tactical approach of the Miguelites was advancing, in the French style, in close columns. Within in range of enemy positions, the attackers would open out in lines to lose potential break-in effect. As a matter of course, this left the Miguelites exposed to hostile defensive fire not more than 50 meters away.

8 -11 September 1832: The Liberal troops, slowly reinforced by the emerging battalions of Porto volunteers repelled minor attacks on Porto and the Serra of Pilar. At the Serra of Pilar, the attack was courageously repulsed by volunteers known as the Serra Poles (*Polacos da Serra*). On the 8 of September, the 5th Light Infantry (Caçadores) Battalion also helped defend the Serra of Pilar, and returned to Porto afterwards, leaving some riflemen together with defenders of the Serra Monastery. Despite all the efforts of Brigadier Torres, commander of the Liberal garrison of the Serra Monastery, he and his 600 men were surrounded in their positions and could not allow the Miguelites to be the full owners of Vila Nova de Gaia.

9 September 1832: The Miguelites bombarded Porto for the first time, commencing a nearly "by-the-clock" routine of harassing the city with heavy artillery fire mainly from 24 and 36 pounder guns, and 6 inch howitzers and mortars. In a few months, a privately purchased heavy gun would arrive in Porto; a 220 mm naval gun, bought by a Miguelite supporter João Paulo Cordeiro. This gun was the object of a vague description, as most historical references describe it as *Paixhans Howitzer Cannon* of French origin. However, William Bollaert, who served in the Liberal Army, described the piece as having been assembled by Scottish foundries. A myth was raised around this gun, which was positioned along the Vila Nova de Gaia heights. Unfortunately, due to poor handling, the cannon was never able to inflict damage to the Liberal held Serra Convent, or to reach long distance targets on the northern banks of the Douro River. After the war, it was taken into Porto as a trophy, but there are no more references to the *Paihxans* gun; it was probably sent to Lisbon to end its days at the Army Royal Arsenal (**see Plate 19**).

Some two and a half miles from the mouth of Douro, the environs of Porto covered a steep hillside that sloped down to the river quays. To the north and east laymore hills, while to the south, across the river, rose a steep cliff on which the Serra of Pilar Convent was built. Below this, across the bridge from Porto, was the long, straggling town of Villa Nova de Gaia where the British wine traders and shippers had their huge warehouses full of maturing Port. More hills lay to the south overlooking Vila Nova and the river. A sand bar restricted the mouth of the river to the south. On the northern bank, at the mouth of the Douro, was the little town of S. João da Foz, known to the British as 'the Foz', where the British community had their summer villas; their beach on the Atlantic coast where they strolled was even then known as the *Praia dos Inglezes* (Englishmen Beach). Overlooking Foz was Luz with its lighthouse and fort and between Foz and Porto was a two-mile long stretch of flat, open country scattered with hamlets and farms, itself overlooked by more high ground.

The other weak point in the defences was the low flat area between Foz and Porto. Once the Miguelites had begun setting up batteries to the south of the Douro, they were effectively able to close the river to shipping, although one or two vessels were still able to get in and out. From late November 1832, any reinforcements or supplies had to be landed on the open beach at the mouth of the Douro or on the northern bank under fire from hostile batteries. Once the enemy batteries were built on the sandbar, the river was closed. Even the Praia dos Inglezes was partially under fire. Rough seas and high winds could make any landing very hazardous or impossible and even when supplies and reinforcements were landed they had to make their way to the city along the two-mile long strip of narrow territory held by the defenders, before they could enter the relative safety of the city. While Foz had its own fort and Luz had powerful fortifications commanded by the able and energetic Colonel José da Fonseca, the open area had only the lightest of entrenchments and a few batteries and strongpoints.

16 September 1832: The besieged Liberals made their first sortie from the city barricades and occupied the Hill of Antas (Morro das Antas or Cerro das Antes), the capture of which would control the high ground of Porto's northern perimeter. This would provide the defenders with a broad view of the Campanhã Valley where, at a relatively short distance, where the 2nd Miguelite Division of approximately 10,000 men was situated. This force, situated along a 5 km front, menaced Porto from the north.

29 September 1832: The Porto defenders repelled a Miguelite attempt to storm the city, and truly the first large scale battle of the Siege of Porto and the Miguelite Wars. On this day the fate of the Liberal movement was placed under a severe test. Indeed, it could have resulted in a decisive defeat for D. Pedro troops and the besieged city of Porto. At dawn and under cover of a thick fog, the Miguelites advanced, in two 5,000 men columns, through the northern outskirts of Porto at 0600/0700 hours and headed for the Campanhã forts and the recently disputed heights of Antas heights. The Miguelite infantry penetrated the perimeters defended by the batteries of the Bonfim, Cativo and Fojo, taking the Lomba battery, defended by the Academic Corps artillerymen, but were violently stopped at the Rua do Prado after they managed to penetrate 1 km inside the city. The Liberal sentinels caught by surprise, retreated, but the alarm was given and all of the Liberal troops available counter attacked the Miguelites in the Mijavelhas field (nowadays 24th August Square) and through the day managed to drove them back to Campanhã Valley at bayonet point. The resulting battle was so fierce that the street was subsequently renamed Heroism Street (Rua do Heroísmo). D. Pedro, himself, was plainly involved in the battle, attending all the combat places and boosting the troops morale, sometimes exposing himself too much. Lieutenant Colonel Pacheco (who would be killed after the siege in a skirmish with retreating Miguelite troops) distinguished himself defending a position between S. Cosme road and the battery of the Barros de Lima heights, keeping and holding the lines with Line Infantry, Caçadores and Volunteers companies. João Nepomuceno de Macedo, a cavalry officer, with 300 to 400 men, held the Miguelite infantry battalions in the Bonfim hills, retaking the fallen batteries (in 1835 Nepomuceno was made Baron of S. Cosme to commemorate his contribution). After more than nine hours of severe combat of heavy defensive musketry and frontal assaults, and having made no significant progress in any position, Miguelite General Gaspar Teixeira de Lacerda called off the attack. The Liberal defenders lost 650 men and the Miguelites about 4,000. This boosted the will of the Liberals to stay in Porto and defend the city. From that day available male citizens were recruited in numbers for the Porto Volunteer Battalions, which were designated with professional designations (ex: Civil Servants Battalion) or local names like the Santo Ovídio Battalion. With the defeat of his first large scale offensive, D. Miguel decided to leave Lisbon and head north in an attempt to raise army about Porto.

13-16 October 1832: The Miguelites completed the encirclement of Porto and had more than 12 heavy artillery batteries situated on the left bank of the Douro. Some were ensconced on the heights of Vila Nova de Gaia. Others were situated on the lower banks to harass the northern bank from the city walls down to the sea, damaging civilian houses, stores, anchored merchant ships and bombarding the river road which was essential to keep open communications with the sea front where almost all of Porto's supplies were landed by night. These included food, weapons, ammunition and volunteer drafts such as the second draft of Belgian troops. This meant that Gaspar Teixeira's lines of siege works were complete around Porto. The Serra Convent Liberal garrison under General Torres, on 16 October, repelled furious attacks of the Miguelite division stationed in the Vila Nova de Gaia outskirts after several hours of heavy bombardment. During this time D. Miguel left for Braga and on 1 November, established his general staff in Braga and replaced General Gaspar Teixeira with Viscount General Santa Marta. With the increased blockade both on land and sea, this led to a dearth of food supplies for Porto. The shortage of goods and

Battle of 29 September 1832. Detail from Colonel Moreira Porto siege lines 1833.

even ammunitions, together with hunger and epidemic diseases began to have an effect the city's defenders and civilian population. However, the former continued to reinforce the defensive perimeter and launch numerous sorties to clear a way for resupply.

11-12 November 1832: On 11 November 1832, the birthday of D. Pedro, the Miguelites started an uninterrupted bombardment of Porto, which lasted until nightfall of the next day, the shells striking houses, churches and sending iron splinters through the streets, killing and injuring civilians and troops alike. However, this bombardment had the reverse effect of that intended, as the civilian population pulled together in support of the Liberal cause, not only by the increased rate of recruits for the City Volunteer Battalions, but also women's efforts to support the defenders, not only by providing water and food at the barricades, but also sewing the volunteers and line troops uniforms or assuming the dangerous task of manufacturing thousands of muskets, carbines and pistol cartridges and transporting the ammunitions to the frontline. Conversely., a continuous shortage of cash to pay troops led to constant mutinies by English mercenaries. This resulted in many departures including Admiral Sartorius who would be replaced by Admiral Napier.

14-17 November 1832: The Miguelite forces repelled the first Liberal sortie in order to extend and seal the most vulnerable positions in the Liberal lines. However, Lieutenant-colonel Silva Pereira distinguished himself when the 5th Caçadores Battalion sortied and stormed the Antas heights. This fragile position, between the great battery and Liberal headquarters of the mount of Quinta dos Congregados on the right, and the battery of Guelas de Pau on the left, was some distance from the Liberal lines. Pereira distinguished himself sufficiently enough to be promoted to full colonel and battalion commander. The Liberals withdrew as the Miguelites managed to repel the sortie, although the Liberal command tried again with more attacks on the Antas heights to secure this extension of the Liberal lines.

28 November-17 December 1832: For almost a month, due to the arrival of more foreign reinforcements and an increase in volunteer battalion numbers, the Liberals launched several more sorties. Miguelite forces repelled those directed against the northern outskirts of Porto. However, the defenders commanded by Brigadier Torres successfully stormed the surrounding Miguelite positions in Vila Nova de Gaia and managed to destroy or damage the hostile gun batteries there.

1 January 1833: For political reasons due to the deep ideological differences within Liberal factions, the internal strife amongst the military command became clear. This resulted in the Duke da Terceira's dismissal as commander of the Liberal Army. Ordered by D. Pedro in a controversial decision, French General Solignac, a veteran of the Napoleonic Wars and Algerian campaigns, was appointed in his place. This occurred despite a certain amount of hostility amongst the rank and file. Most of January 1833 was a daily routine of Miguelite bombardments and reinforcement of their three largest Atlantic forts (Crasto, Ervilha and Serralves). This threatened the Liberal lines astride the northern bank of the Douro River and risked the cutting of all supply supplies brought by way of the Ouro road. It was clear that the Liberals should reinforce the sector, so as to avoid Porto's isolation from the sea. This was because all war and merchant ships were under threat of Miguelite batteries situated on the southern river bank, sinking or damaging some schooners and brigs whilst these vessels made their way out to sea. The remaining vessels were 3 British warships detached by HM Government to evacuate the British businessmen and their families.

24 January 1833: The Miguelites frustrated an attack on their lines to the northwest of Porto. This occurred at the forts of Crasto and Queijo (literally "Cheese"). According to Lovell who was present at the time:

> The Marshal determined on attacking the right of the Miguelite position; indeed, to cut off the right towards the fort of Queijo. The fleet were to act in combination: however, they did not get to their stations in time, and Sartorius's crew had mutinied and refused to weigh anchor. At three P.M. the attack on the land side commenced. After a severe action the Miguelites were driven back some little distance, and the height called Castro in front of the lighthouse was taken. The troops nearly reached Queixo Castle, but the Miguelites stood fast at Lordello; and a second attack, which the Marshal had ordered, did not take place; countermanded, it is said, by the Emperor, who feared to endanger the city. The Marshal, finding that the attack upon the enemy's right did not cause the Miguelites to weaken their centre, fell back after dark, and with considerable loss to his old ground; much disheartened on finding his support doubtful, and his French troops not quite equal to the veterans of Napoleon. Indeed, the Miguelites drove them

back more than once, and the French found themselves opposed to the old regiments who, under the Duke of Wellington and Marshal Beresford, had learned to beat them.[1]

28 January 1833: Under pressure from the Constitutionalists (Liberals left wing), and much to the consternation of D. Pedro, the celebrated General Saldanha arrived at Porto with a faction of Liberal extremists. D. Pedro, despite his personal animosity towards the general, promoted Saldanha to Marshal, and gave him the command of the 2nd division, but in fact of the whole of the Liberal Army, since Solignac, due to his excessive caution in taking offensive actions, especially in the Lordelo sector, was losing the trust of D. Pedro. Ultimately Solignac asked to be dismissed, and subsequently left Portugal.

Saldanha was the chief figure from now on, providing strong support for all Liberal strategies with regard to Porto's defence. Part of this approach concerned a scheme to attack Lisbon. During the last days of January, the Miguelites continued to bombard Porto town and re-occupied Monte Castro fort from which they had been driven during the last sortie. Further to this, siege works were reinforced in that sector, in order to avoid another perimeter breach. Marshal Saldanha immediately reacted, ordering the construction of more batteries in the Pasteleiro hills opposite the three huge forts of Castro, Ervilha and Serralves. In addition to extending Liberal lines in order to relieve pressure on the river road, he ordered Colonel Shaw and his English and Scottish troops to establish positions within the Pasteleiro lines. Despite their reputation for disorderly conduct within Porto, they were one of the best of the foreign raised corps, and it was with regularity that they assaulted the Miguelite forts.[2]

4-6 February 1833: A *Cholera Morbus* epidemic with a likely origin from Belgian troops who landed in January, broke out amongst the inhabitants of Porto. British troops mutinied for more pay.[3]

21 February 1833: The Count of S. Lourenço was appointed to the command the Miguelite forces. A fierce supporter of the Absolutist regime, he increased the attacks and daily bombardments not only against Porto's defensive works but also on civilian quarters. The situation in the city was becoming more and more difficult, with a dearth of food and firewood being the most significant of problems. Popular narratives of the time report that Porto's inhabitants developed imaginative recipes of rice, sugar, and salted cod after consumption of beef and pork stores. It was not long before dogs and cats disappeared. Fishing in the Douro became a tricky business with those who attempted to do so offering tempting targets to Miguelite sharpshooters. The situation was so desperate that some of politicians and a few army officers considered capitulating or at least returning to the fleet and ultimately to the Azores. Saldanha strongly opposed this, as did D. Pedro despite their mutual antipathy. At the time, the Miguelite Army surrounding Porto was as follows:

1 Lovell Badcock, *Rough leaves from a Journal kept in Spain and Portugal, during the years 1832, 1833 and 1834.* (London: ed. Richard Bentley, New Burlington Street, 1835). pp.189-90.
2 Badcock, *Rough leaves from a Journal kept in Spain and Portugal, during the years 1832, 1833 and 1834,* p. 192
3 Badcock, *Rough leaves from a Journal kept in Spain and Portugal, during the years 1832, 1833 and 1834,* p. 194

Miguelite Army during the Siege of Porto – 17 February 1833					
Divisions	**Branches**	**Troops**	**Horses**	**Artillery**	
				Field Guns	**Howitzers**
2nd Division North of Douro River	Artillery	153	118	5	2
	Cavalry	540	422	-	-
	4 Infantry Line Regiments and 1 Caçadores Battalion	7135	-	-	-
	8 Royalist Volunteers Battalions	3609	-	-	-
	7 Militia Regiments	3615	-	-	-
	Total	**15052**	**540**	**5**	**2**
4th Division North of Douro River	Artillery	295	216	6	2
	Cavalry	654	332	-	
	4 Infantry Line Regiments and 1 Caçadores Battalion	4881	-	-	-
	7 Royalist Volunteers Battalions	2599	85		
	6 Militia Regiments	3394			
	Total	**11823**	**633**	**6**	**2**
Mobile Column	Artillery	47	21	2	1
	Cavalry	119	100		
	1 Infantry Line Regiment	817			
	2 Royalist Volunteers Battalions	507			
	2 Militia Regiments	1147			
	Total	**2637**	**121**	**2**	**1**
3rd Division South of Douro River	Artillery	108	82	3	1
	Cavalry	486	381		
	3 Infantry Line Regiments and 1 Caçadores Battalion	2611			
	5 Royalist Volunteers Battalions	1968			
	9 Militia Regiments	4824			
	Total	**9997**	**463**	**3**	**1**
Total of the Siege Miguelite forces		**39509**	**1787**	**16**	**6**

Artillery	603	437		
13 Cavalry Squadrons	1799	1235		
14 Line Regiments and 2 Caçadores Battalions	15444			
22 Royalists Volunteers Battalions	8683	85		
24 Militia Regiments	12980			
Total	**35509**	**1757**	**16**	**6**

Note: The Miguelite siege artillery is not included in this chart.

2-24 March 1833: During March the Liberals repelled successive Miguelite assaults on the lines to the east and northwest of Porto. Almost every day an attack by infantry, caçadores, cavalry and Royalist volunteers with artillery support, became routine for the city's defenders. In early March, Colonel Pereira, commander of the 5th Caçadores, was given command of the 2nd brigade of 1st division. This unit consisted of regular light troops and volunteers. Two days after his promotion, the Miguelites commenced daily attacks on Porto in an attempt to wear the exhausted defenders out. Many spent days on the ramparts where they maintained permanent sentry duty, taking meagre meals provided by wives and relatives. Others occupied the palisades, distributing ammunition and fresh water whilst being exposed to musket fire and bombardments. Ammunition shortages had become serious since the Douro was closed by Miguelite batteries. By then all supplies had to be brought ashore by small boats and transported by pack columns marching in complete silence , through covered ways along the Douro. Their loads included food, musket cartridges, gunpowder, flints and other vital supplies. More often than not, these columns were shelled despite maintenance of silence.

4 March 1833: At dawn, the Miguelites launched a feint attack in the direction of Aguardente and Bomfim redoubts. At 0700 hours the Miguelite infantry assailed the Pasteleiro and Lordelo lines supported by the fire from the Castro and Ervilha e Serralves batteries. The Miguelite regiments followed the tactic of charging in close packed columns, but a short distance from the city defensive lines, they opened ranks and charged forward in packed columns. However, a short distance from the city lines, the attackers opened ranks thus losing their punching power. Confronted by murderous Liberal volleys, they were driven back to their trenches. Simultaneously, a heavy Miguelite assault was launched against the Serra Convent, Defeated by murderous grapeshot fire from the Liberal battery situated within the convent, by mid-day, the exchange of fire began to die down before settling down to sporadic episodes for the remainder of the day.

13 March 1833: Disaffection amongst the Liberal high command and troop payment problems led to Admiral Sartorius dismissal.

16 March 1833: The Iberian Peninsula was in a political turmoil as Liberals and Absolutists descended into fratricidal conflict. These troubles being closely monitored by Great Britain, France and Austria, the absolutist pretender to the Spanish throne, Don Carlos of Spain, arrived in Portugal with troops intended to join D. Miguel's forces. This raised the risk of the conflict spreading beyond the Portuguese-Spanish border. Indeed, this would happen in 1835 during the First Carlist War.

23 March 1833: The Miguelite forces commenced further offensive action against Porto in an attempt to exploit defensive weaknesses. On 23 March their infantry advanced under cover and made a surprise attack upon an outwork near the Aguardente battery a and destroyed it. Skirmishers entered the Liberal lines, some of which pressed on to the heights near the Bomfim positions. The hard-pressed Liberals regrouped and, reacting quickly, launched a sortie to retake this point, which, after considerable loss on both sides, was accomplished and the Miguelites were driven back. Simultaneous attacks were made upon Foz and the Pasteleiro, but both failed due to the determined resistance of English and Scottish troops, as well as Portuguese units under the command of Colonel Shaw. Despite this, the fighting lasted until the next day, the preceding night consisting of exchanges of musketry between the advanced post garrisons and forward patrols.

24 March 1833: Colonel Pereira and the 5th Caçadores Battalion intrepidly attacked the Antas heights, This compelled the enemy to abandon it for good, thus removing the Miguelites from an advantageous position over the northern Liberal lines. They went on to repel two counter attacks by superior numbers. As a result, Pereira became a knight of the order of the Tower and Sword.,

5 April 1833: Being Good Friday, one of the most important dates on the Christian calendar both Catholic and Protestant, the flags of the contending armies were hung at half-mast on forts and redoubts; white for Miguelite, and blue and white for the Liberals. For one day, the guns were silenced and combatants and civilians could leave ramparts or shelter without danger. The siege routine commenced the next day.

8–9 April 1833: Covelo Hill was a well-fortified Miguelite salient a few hundred metres from the Liberal lines of Aguardente and Lindo Vale. Situated in the Paranhos valley, its Miguelite garrison was more than a kilometre from their own lines. This was an unsustainable position, because of the close proximity of a Miguelite fort and the constant threat of Liberal assaults into weak points within the Miguelite defensive works. For D. Pedro, known for his daily inspections, this was a scandalous state of affairs as far as the engineers were concerned. For the Duke of Bragança, something had to be done to solve the awkward situation. On 8 April, the Liberal batteries from Aguardente to Sério opened heavy fire on the Miguelite redoubt on Covelo Hill with the intention to storm it with light troops. The attempt failed, so an infantry assault was ordered for the next day.

9 April 1833: Despite heavy bombardment of the previous day that left the Miguelites almost unscathed, the Liberals launched an audacious sortie and stormed the Covelo redoubt at bayonet point. Surviving Miguelite troops withdrew towards Paranhos. Liberal Caçadores battalions were involved in the attack as well a as infantry sappers who were tasked with spiking the Miguelite cannons in the off-chance that it was impossible to hold the objective. Lovell subsequently observed:

> The Miguelites made an attack to the right to divert our attention; they afterwards abandoned the heights of Covelho, upon its being menaced, and it was taken possession of without loss. Why the Miguelites did not defend it, having the village of Paranhas immediately behind them, I cannot imagine.[4]

4 Badcock, *Rough leaves from a Journal kept in Spain and Portugal, during the years 1832, 1833 and 1834*, p. 230.

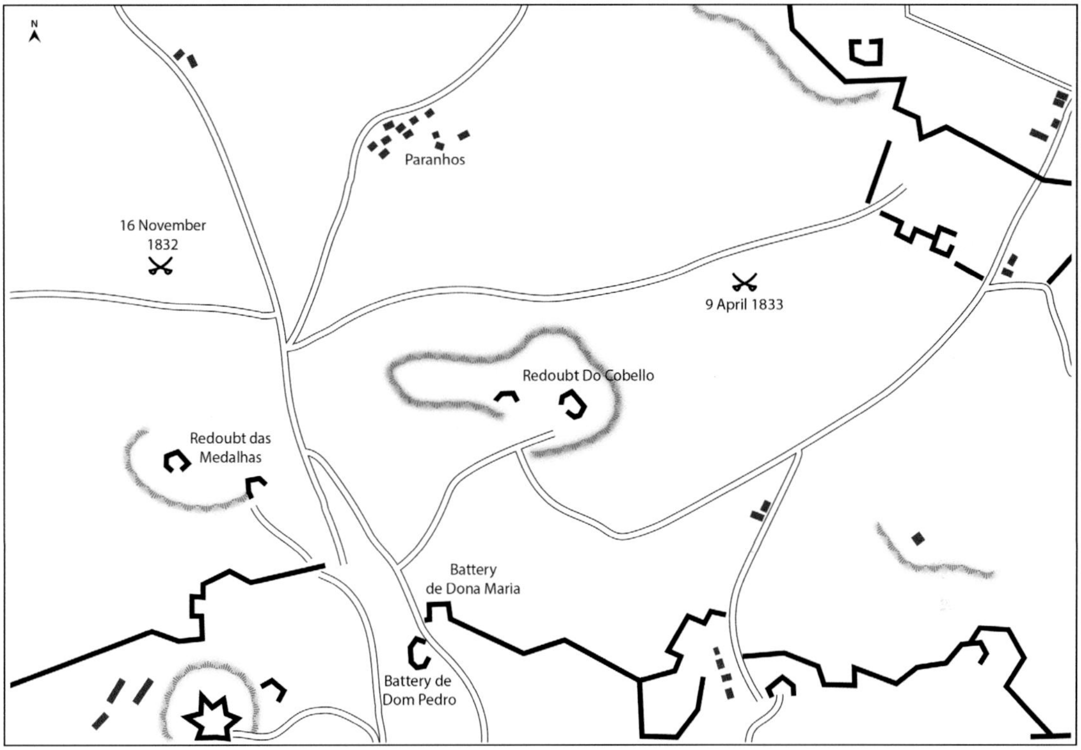

9 April 1833 Battle for Covello.

10 April 1833: The importance maintaining the Covelo position became clear on 10 April. Regrouping units from the large infantry encampment situated on the S. Mamede de Infesta plain, the Miguelites planned to retake Covelo. At dawn, a desperate attempt to recapture the hill was beaten back in a savage hand-to-hand engagement, the Liberal Caçadores and volunteers, taking advantage of the confusion amongst the enemy ranks to advance towards the village of Paranhos after a bitter fight. To disperse the Liberal forces, but also demonstrating the importance of Covelo Hill, the Miguelites were simultaneously threatening the positions at Foz, Lordello, and Vanzeller Farm. However, they failed in every place. The British and Scottish, under Shaw's command, suffered much during an attack to keep the Lordelo road to Porto open.

15-25 April 1833: Although the Liberals retained Portuguese commanders like Saldanha, they also had experienced foreign officers such as Shaw, Bollaert, Napier, Timmermans, Omboni and St. Léger, all of whom were key figures. In addition to commanding British, Scottish, French, Belgians, and Italians, they also assisted their Portuguese counterparts with training Mobiles and volunteer battalions. Many of the Mobile battalions were from outside Porto. For example, the Minho battalion hailed from Braga, Penafiel, Guimarães, etc. Other Mobile units had left northern Portugal to campaign in the south, thus providing substantial Liberal Army reinforcements.

Viscount and General Santa Marta, a Miguelite Army commander. (National Library of Portugal)

D. Miguel, exhausted by the continuous quarrels between his generals such as Álvaro Xavier da Fonseca Coutinho e Póvoas, Santa Marta, or Lacerda, thought that appointment of a foreigner would be the solution ot the increased deadlock about Porto and the Convento da Serra redoubt. D. Miguel, aware of the incompetence of some of his generals, was greatly concerned about the menace of the growing Liberal movement throughout Portugal, especially in Lisbon and the coastal ports, As the interior was more conservative and prone to the Miguelite cause, the choice was a former officer of Napoleon's army and conquerer of Algeria who had fallen into disgrace for his conservative politics after defeat at the celebrated Paris barricades of 1830. This General Louis Auguste Victor de Ghaisne de Bourmont arrived in Portugal in April 1833 with a secret brief from the Holy Alliance to advise and assist D. Miguel with the Porto siege operations – a prerequisite for Holy Alliance acknowledgment of D. Miguel.

1 May 1833: The continuous unrest in the Liberal naval squadron was a daily concern to D. Pedro and his commanding officers. Following the Liberal squadron mutiny at Vigo, Admiral Sartorius was reinstated as fleet commander. The mutinous sailors having been paid off and returned to duty, the squadron departed for the northern coast of Portugal under threat of the Miguelite fleet.

About Porto and the Convent of Serra, the month of May was one of daily bombardments without major engagements, the only action being that of exchanges between opposing pickets and reconnaissances by both sides. The loss of Covelo Hill ensured that the plains and farms of Paranhos valley were under fire from Liberal batteries.

A Bold Move: Liberal Expedition to Algarve

1 June 1833: The Duke de Palmela, D. Pedro's ambassador in London, and Admiral Charles Napier arrived at Porto with reinforcements of mostly foreign troops including 600 Belgians. For the first time the Liberals began to realize that an offensive outside Porto could relieve pressure on the city, especially since the troop strength increased from 8,300 to nearly 13,000 men. Although this was not a great advantage when facing a Miguelite army of 40,000 men, a plan to attack an objective far from the besieged city could divide the opposing Miguelite divisions. Thus Napier advised the resurrection of a shelved plan for a surprise seaborne assault on Lisbon, which was later modified to a landing at Algarve. This expedition was to be carried out by a small force of 2,500 commanded by the Duke of Terceira, his force to be transported by Napier's naval squadron.

8 June 1833: Following the growing conflict betwwen D. Pedro and Sartorius,Napier was appointed admiral of the Liberal squadron. Further to this, Saldanha was appointed chief of the general staff, in reality supreme commander of the Liberal Army in all Portugal. Adhering to the plan to take the conflict beyond Porto, the Duke of Terceira was appointed commander of the southern expedition to be accompanied by Napier's naval squadron. Pedro de Sousa Holstein, Duke of Palmela was appointed civil governor of Porto. The major effort to prepare an expedition of an under sized brigade, packed into a transport steamers and escorted by a small fleet in which the most powerful warships were one 48 gun frigate and two 46 and 42 gun frigates. Sailing along the Portuguese coast to Algarve, the risk of being intercepted by the far superior Miguelite fleet was great. Under constant harassment of the Miguelite batteries, the Liberal fleet approached the S. João da Foz and board 2,500 men and supplies before sailing for Algarve. All this occurred whilst deceiving the Miguelite command in nearby Porto. The deception caused them to believe the force would depar for Lisbon prior to being crushed by capital garrisons or sunk by the Miguelite fleet. The Liberal plan was bold and daring and managed to keep its real intention secret.

24 June 1833: Following the plan, the 2,500 Liberal troops commanded by the Duke of Terceira, landed in the Algarve at Cacela Velha near Monte Gordo. Encountering no resistance, the Liberal brigade occupied Tavira before marching north through the Alentejo. Unexpectedly, they also did not meet significant resistance in the towns and countryside. In fact, quite the reverse, since several garrison and militia regiments from the Alentejo joined the Liberal forces which were now marching towards Lisbon as rapidly as possible. So it was that when the Liberal forces arrived at Setúbal on the south bank of the River Tagus, it was a far superior force that surprised the astonished Miguelite garrison.

4 July 1833: The Liberal expedition to south Portugal left Porto without difficulty, the only hostile response being artillery fire from the Vila Nova de Gaia Miguelite batteries. The latter continued bombard key Liberal positions, primarily the river roads and Antas heights. At 1300, the Miguelites launched an assault on the Lordelo redoubts. The attack then extended along the Pasteleiro front with the Miguelites making a strong effort to seize Vanzeller Farm stronghold and the Mirante Battery defended by French and Belgian troops of the Portuguese *Tiralleurs* Battalion, as well as Portuguese Caçadores troops. Their commander, Colonel Duvergier, charged the Miguelites at the head of the French infantry and repulsed them. Having reached the farm garden walls, it was during this action that Duvergier lost his arm and subsequently died of amputation complications on 23 July.

The Miguelites also made an attack on the Bonfim battery, storming a piquet house, and got within the precincts of the former Marshal Saldanha, who was nearby inspecting positions with his staff, accompanied by no more than 25 men, charged the Miguelite infantry and drove them back at sword point. A heavy cannonade was maintained on the city by almost every Miguelite battery north and south the Douro. Artillery and musket fire died down at 1700 hours. The defenders lost 130 men and the Miguelites likely more, but there are no definitive numbers available. Lieutenant-Colonel Lovell Badcock, in the Liberal Army Service, believed it was a large reconnaissance in force made by numerous pickets instead of a serious attack because there were no discernable assault columns. The defenders, however, viewed the repulse as a great victory, ringing bells rang and sanctioning bonfires.

Liberal Success in the South – Battle of Cape St. Vincent and Terceira's Advance through Alentejo

5 July 1833: On 5 July 1833, the Liberal squadron under Admiral Napier seized the Miguelite fleet at the battle of Cape St. Vincent (Cabo São Vincente). Napier's force was only a squadron of 6 ships: 3 ex-merchantmen converted frigates, a corvette, a brig, and a schooner, mounting a total of 176 guns. This force provided escort for the Duke of Terceira troop transports. Napier also had some small steamers that he hoped to employ as tugboats. Cape St. Vincent in sight, the Liberal squadron encountered the Miguelite fleet. On 5 July, the wind got up and at 0400 hours, in full sail, and avoiding an enemy envelopment, Napier ordered an attack on the hostile fleet of 3 ships of the line, a frigate, a xebec, 3 corvettes and 2 brigs, mounting a total of 372 guns. Well aware that he could not expose his ships to superior gunfire, Napier ordered his ships to close with the enemy before boarding. Thus, the battle was decided by hand-to-hand fighting with muskets, pistols, cutlasses and pikes. With this bold move the Liberal fleet captured all three ships of the line, a frigate, and a corvette, the crews agreeing to fight from now on for Dona Maria II. The remnants of the Miguelite fleet fled to Lisbon or Madeira. Napier's casualties were some 30 killed, including the captain of the *Rainha de Portugal* and two other captains, and approximately 60 wounded as opposed to 200-300 of the enemy including Miguelite Admiral Manuel António Marreiros. On 6 July, D. Pedro bestowed on Napier the title of Viscount Cape St. Vincent in the peerage of Portugal. Following this, Napier's fleet was ravaged by cholera, simultaneously raging in Porto, with huge loss of life. He was, however, able to return to Lisbon, now hastily abandoned to Terceira's expeditionary force, with squadron and captured vessels intact. For his part, Terceira had advanced from the Algarve, crossed the Alentejo before arriving at the southern bank of the Tagus. There his force defeated the Miguelites at the Battle of Almada. The river passage secured, Terceira prepared to occupy Lisbon. Meanwhile, at Porto, having witnessed the departure of the Liberal fleet, the Miguelites believed that the city defences were seriously weakened. A series of attacks launched on 5 July, the same day as the Battle of Cape of St. Vincent, resulted in defeat of the Miguelite columns with heavy losses.

14 July 1833: Finally, to the Portuguese Miguelite high command's dismay, General Bourmont was personally appointed chief of Porto's Miguelite army. Bourmont, relying on his previous Algerian experience, was well aware of the growing logistic difficulties following the recent defeat of the Miguelite fleet, as well as unrest to the point of mutiny amongst the garrison due to badly handled sorties and mounting losses. Bourmont was also aware that the Duke of Terceira's expedition was rapidly advancing through Alentejo and reaching Lisbon. His best troops around Porto and to the south, Bourmont had to finish with Porto in order to move south to reinforce the Lisbon garrisons. Except for some line regiments, most of his troops were undisciplined Royalist volunteers and guerrilla bands. Other concerns for Bourmont and his staff was intelligence that the Liberals in south were advancing against weak resistance and, more surprisingly, a

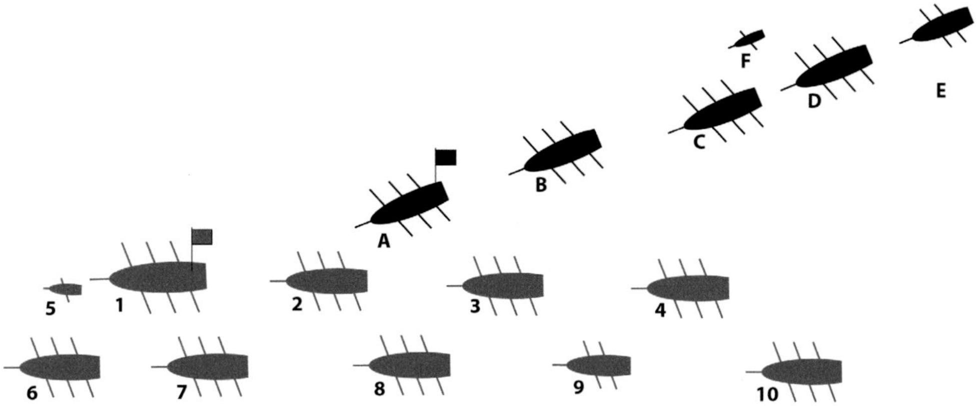

Dona Maria Fleet

A. *Rainha de Portugal,* Flagship, frigate 46 guns
B. *Dom Pedro (ex-Wellington),* frigate 48 guns
C. *Dona Maria,* frigate 42 guns
D. *Portuense,* corvette 18 guns
E. *Villa Flor,* brig 16 guns
F. *Faro,* schooner 6 guns

Total 176 guns

Dom Miguel Fleet

1. *Dom João 6º,* ship of the line 80 guns
2. *Rainha,* ship of the line 76 guns
3. *Martim de Freitas,* ship of the line 48 guns
4. *Princeza Real,* frigate 56 guns
5. Cutter (no other detail)
6. *Isabel Maria,* brig 24 guns
7. *Tejo,* brig 20 guns
8. *Princeza Real,* corvette 22 guns
9. *Audaz,* brig 20 guns
10. *Cybelle,* corvette 26 guns

Total 372 guns

Admiral Sir Charles Napier's attack plan.

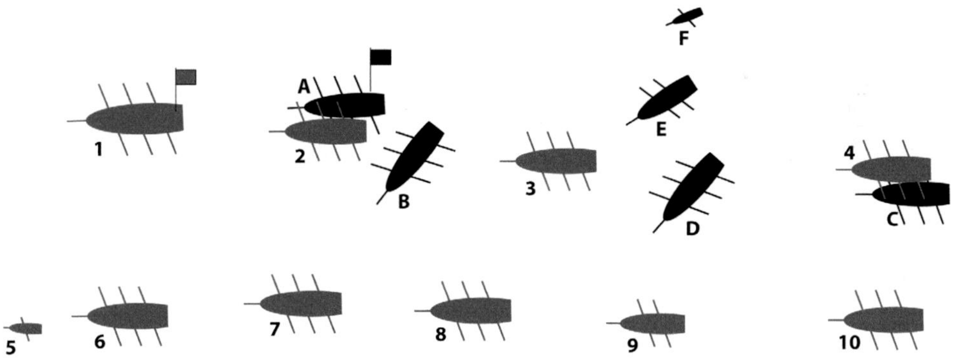

Dona Maria Fleet

A. *Rainha de Portugal,* Flagship, frigate 46 guns
B. *Dom Pedro (ex-Wellington),* frigate 48 guns
C. *Dona Maria,* frigate 42 guns
D. *Portuense,* corvette 18 guns
E. *Villa Flor,* brig 16 guns
F. *Faro,* schooner 6 guns

Total 176 guns

Dom Miguel Fleet

1. *Dom João 6º,* ship of the line 80 guns
2. *Rainha,* ship of the line 76 guns
3. *Martim de Freitas,* ship of the line 48 guns
4. *Princeza Real,* frigate 56 guns
5. Cutter (no other detail)
6. *Isabel Maria,* brig 24 guns
7. *Tejo,* brig 20 guns
8. *Princeza Real,* corvette 22 guns
9. *Audaz,* brig 20 guns
10. *Cybelle,* corvette 26 guns

Total 372 guns

Attack and boarding of the enemy fleet by the Liberal Squadron.

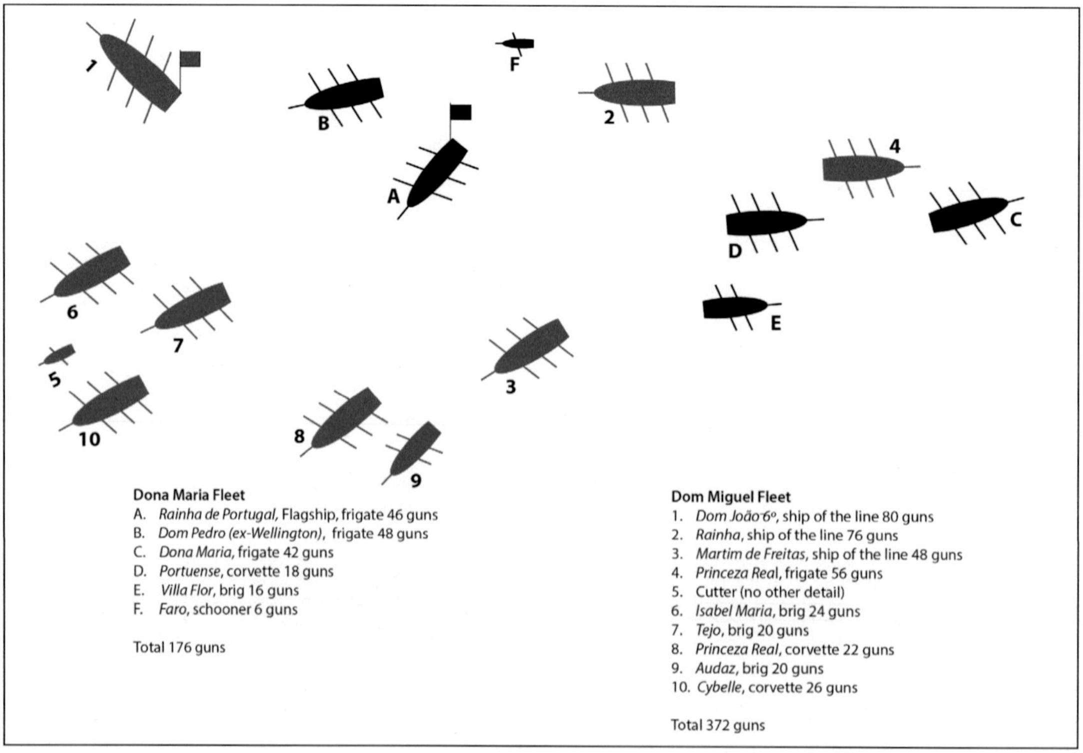

Ship positions following the battle.

considerable amount of desertions amongst Terceira's Miguelite units. Bourmont was running out of time. so a decisive offensive had to be launched against Porto.

23 July 1833: The reinforced Liberals defeated the Miguelites near Almada at the action of Cova da Piedade. This was an open battle as opposed to a siege engagement. It was there that the Liberals, now numbering some 4,000 men, met the Miguelite generals Duke of Cadaval and Teles Jordão with 3,000 regular infantry and 3 cavalry squadrons and some batteries of light artillery pieces. The superior fire discipline of the Liberal forces, delivering murderous volleys, threw back the panicked Miguelites, and Jordão, notorious for personal hatred of Liberals and his numerous atrocities against them, was captured and slain.

Despite his victory, Terceira was in a difficult position. He had to cross the Tagus at its widest point, and was aware that another Miguelite division was approaching from the south under the command of the Baron Molelos. This movement would threaten any attempt to retreat by the Liberal army. Moreover, on the north side of the Tagus was the main force of the Duke of Cadaval with 12,000 men supported by artillery waiting for Terceira. A movement by either side was likely to be decisive considering that Terceira was isolated by the riverbanks and Napier's vessels could not enter the Tagus due to prevailing winds that closed off the river bar. However, it would be Cadaval who sealed Lisbon's fate.

In Lisbon, all of D. Miguel ministers were utterly shocked by the Liberal victory of Cova da Piedade and the death of Jordão along with the worse news of Cape St. Vincent and the surrender of half the Miguelite squadron. The enemy's fleet eliminated, Admiral Napier could blockade Lisbon without interruption by major naval threat. The Duke of Cadaval, recognizing that it was a question of hours before favourable winds allowed Napier's ships to enter the Tagus, advised immediate withdrawal from Lisbon towards Loures, a village near the old ramparts of the Peninsular War Lines of Torres Vedras. Thus the Duke of Terceira had an open path to Lisbon. Crossing in Cacilhas on the road to the Lisbon docks on the Tagus River, Terceira's advance was likely that described by Lovell (1835) in that it immediately predates the Liberal entry into Lisbon: '...making a most rapid march, arrived near the Tagus, defeated the corps opposed to him (commanded by Telles Jordaö who was slain.').[5]

Liberal Army on Two Fronts – Conquest of Lisbon and the end of the Siege of Porto

24 July 1833: At last, a year after D. Pedro's army landed between Mindelo and Arnosa and entered Porto, the Liberals were marching on Lisbon. The Duke of Terceira entered Lisbon as the Miguelite garrison withdrew, together with Miguelite ministers and their families and clergy. Fear of retribution for D. Miguel's harsh regime was the primary motivation for the hasty departure. Lacking the latest news from Porto where D. Miguel headquarters remained outside the besieged city, Terceira's major concern was the defence of Lisbon.

25 July 1833: Miguelite attempts to erect effective batteries on the northern outskirts of Lisbon or the ability to launch effective assaults went badly, although all the military resources were available. The Miguelite lines, north of Lisbon and in the vicinity of Santarém, were eventually strengthened, the newly established batteries dominating Lisbon, but it took a great deal of time to achieve this. One explanation for the delay was lack of competent officers, especially engineers. This may explain Miguelite reliance on indiscriminate shelling of the city, a tactic which backfired as far as British and European public opinion was concerned. For its part, the British government certainly turned a blind eye to the clandestine recruitment of soldiers in Britain. The 25 July 1833 saw the last great Miguelite offensive against Porto. It was also Bourmont's first major operation since his appointment. During the night of 24/25 July, the Miguelite began to mass infantry, cavalry, and Caçadores, supported by artillery, opposite weak points in the city's defences; specifically opposite positions from Lordelo to Vanzeller Farm. All of this occurred in total silence. That same night, Marshal Saldanha was inspecting the Liberal lines nearby when he heard the creaking of gun carriages. Saldanha quickly determined that an enemy offensive was in the offing after days of calm. Gathering as much local intelligence as possible, he ordered reinforcements to points he thought were the targets of the impending assault.

Soon after 0500, the Miguelites rushed forward in a desperate attack against the Lordelo lines and Vanzeller Farm.[6] At Lordelo, Miguelite cavalry squadrons approached through a small wood at slow pace. Then, at the sound of a bugler, they jumped a stone wall and galloped towards the Liberal lines. The cavalry commander, a French officer, was killed by a musket volley that stalled the attack before the road objective was reached.

Elsewhere, Miguelite infantry stormed a Liberal position only to lose it again. For their part, the Miguelites also assaulted Vanzeller Farm several times before being bloodily repulsed. The new Miguelite

5 Badcock, *Rough leaves from a Journal kept in Spain and Portugal, during the years 1832, 1833 and 1834*, p. 307.

6 Badcock, *Rough leaves from a Journal kept in Spain and Portugal, during the years 1832, 1833 and 1834*, p. 328.

battery at Furada fired the entire time in an attempt to engage the Liberal positions at Lordelo. Meantime, cannonades by batteries of both sides, employing solid shot, bombs, and canister, continued unabated. Moreover, Congréve rockets were discharged by a Liberal battery, crewed by British and Portuguese personnel, with great success, terrifying the enemy infantry and cavalry.

At 0900 hours, the Miguelites attacked Bomfim. Saldanha personally assumed command of the defence. The Miguelite aasault column had just reached the entrance to Bomfin when he charged at the head of his staff and 20 lancers of Bacon's Regiment. The unexpected rush of Liberal cavalry, the lancers being most effective, drove the startled Miguelite column back in complete disorder. By 1400 hours the cannonade gradually died down with the attackers having been driven off in complete disorder. This was a major setback for Bourmont, his plans to seize Porto in ruins. The failure was partly based on poor intelligence about weak points in the enemy line. Losses to D. Pedro's forces amounted to approximately 300-400; Miguelites casualties were estimated at some 2,000 men.

26 July 1833: After Sadanha's victory, and despite a few Miguelite units still retaining certain positions outside of Porto, D. Pedro left the city for Lisbon by sea. Following this, Terceira and Napier assumed responsibility for defence of the capital. Both were aware that the Miguelite Army was far from being defeated. Indeed, there were thousands of Miguelite soldiers and volunteers throughout the country. All were eager to fight, as their units marched to Lisbon and Santarém. Saldanha remained in command at Porto, still at full alert because the northern Miguelite regiments did not receive orders to move south. Instead, they remained in the northern provinces of Minho and Trás os Monte because D. Miguel still believed that his forces, the regiments from Trás-os-Montes and Beiras inclusive, could retake Lisbon.

28 July 1833: D. Pedro arrival in Lisbon and was greeted with great joy by the inhabitants. The event was also a morale booster for the Liberal army then in the process raising Lisbon volunteer battalions. The Liberals cause now now controlled both of Portugal's major cities, Lisbon and Porto, where they controlled a sizeable force of more than 16,000 men with more raised every day. In addition to this, they also had access to the Royal Arsenal artillery reserves.

Conversely, the Miguelites controlled the rural areas where they were supported by the aristocracy and a peasantry galvanized by the ultraconservative Catholic Church. A stalemate of nine months ensued. During this time, Dona Maria da Glória was proclaimed Queen with D. Pedro as regent. The latter wasted no time in dismissing the Miguelite ministers and appropriating church property by means ofnew legislation written by Mouzinho da Silveira.

The Liberal Government decreed that they would tolerate the existence of such places until the death of the last friar or nun. Moreover, many convents and monasteries were converted for military use. For example, the Convent of Serra was declared by Queen Dona Maria II to be a first class war fortress. For the next 180 years, the Serra Convent Barracks was the home of one of most important artillery regiments in Portugal.

4 August 1833: Heading south, the Miguelite heavy artillery departed from Porto. This was clear sign to the defenders that D. Miguel's troops were in a poor military situation as far as Lisbon and Santarém were concerned. The Porto defenders morale boosted by this, Saldanha reverted to active military operations, assaulting the Miguelite positions outside the city and forcing them back. However, the Miguelites resisted fiercely despite the pressure, their artillery managing to carry on with the daily routine of shelling. This proved less effective because of the departure of the heavy 36 and 24 pounder guns.

9 August 1833: D. Miguel and his general staff, at last aware of growing Liberal power in Lisbon, concluded they had no other choice but to head south. Frenchman Count Almer was left in command of the the besiegers, who abandoned some siegeworks, but maintained operations from more distant positions. Meanwhile, a serious blow to the D. Miguel faction came from London when HM Government recognized Dona Maria II as Queen of Portugal. This was a clear sign that England would politically intervene in the Iberian Peninsula, since the situation was becoming increasingly worse between the Spanish Liberals of Princess Cristina and the Absolutists of D. Carlos. Both were in receipt of Portuguese support and even had troops inside Portugal. This violation of sovereign territory was granted by both Pedro and D. Miguel. For Miguel, his army's manpower strength weakening day by day, the arrival of ally D. Carlos and his Carlist forces was a welcome reinforcement. Saldanha was keen to have Cristino's Spanish troops in order to pursue the Carlist forces. The situation was alarming to the governments of England and France both of which were concerned that the entire Iberian Peninsula might descend into civil war with serious implications for the rest of Europe.

16 August 1833: At 1200 hours, an enormous explosion succeeded by smaller discharges, enveloped the Vila Nova de Gaiastore warehouses of the English and Portuguese port wine companies. The owners, who were suspected of Miguelite sympathies, sustained great financial loss in the fire that followed. Supposedly ordered by Almer, it was a deliberate act of sabotage by the retreating Miguelites. According to Lovell, it was Bollaert or Owen who ordered the destruction. That afternoon, the Miguelites began to retire from north of the Douro. Based on the assumption that retreat from the city was imminent, Saldanha prepared to intercept the anticipated withdrawal. His plan was to surprise and cut off the Miguelite rear on the Areosa plain which was situated near the northern outskirts of Porto.

18 August 1833: Miguelite forces commenced the withdrawal from Porto after nightfall. During the night of 17/18 August, they marched around the north side of the city before falling back to the Valongo heights. Most of the available artillery was abandoned during this time. Liberal skirmishing companies, reconnoitering after daybreak, encountered some piquet posts and a few occupied redoubts. Fort Areosa had only 200-300 occupants. Despite this, the Miguelite army withdrew from post to post in good order whilst inflicting some loss on the Liberal pursuers. Some failed to escape. Colonel Dodgin and his British battalion surrounded the garrison of one redoubt before persuading them to surrender. The skirmishing continued until 1200 hours with little loss of life.

20-21 August 1833: The Siege of Porto was over. During the night of 20/21 August, the Miguelites retired from Vila Nova de Gaia. By dawn of the 21st, the Liberals occupied it, relieving the year-long besieged garrison of Brigadier Torres in the Serra Convent. Saldanha returned to Porto in triumph thus establishing himself in the role of successful military leader and future politician. Confronting a growing crisis in the north and south, D. Miguel's army advanced on Lisbon from Coimbra.

The War of the Two Brothers in Southern Portugal

25 August-October 1833: The Duke of Terceira entered Lisbon on 24 July and a month later, on 25 August, was under siege by the Miguelites on the north outskirts of the capital where the Liberals erected defensive works, The most active period of the siege occurred during 5-14 September, but the Liberal lines held their against a series of attacks by infantry and cavalry supported by the heavy guns recently arrived from Porto. The Liberal army was also well equipped with heavy guns and mortars with which they responded to the enemy cannonade in kind.

Already in Lisbon, and free to seize the initiative, Marshal Saldanha ordered a sortied by several divisions on 10 October. This lifted the siege, and forced the Miguelites to withdraw eastwards towards Santarém. This moved the front to Ribatejo. The Civil War had now transformed in a year's time from siege operations to a series of pitched battles on a Napoleonic scale. The Liberal Army increased to almost 50,000 men, most of them of regular infantry regiments and Caçadores battalions, with former Miguelite units, the famous Queen's Own Volunteers, now raised to two regiments, several foreign battalions or regiments of British, Scottish, French, Belgians (the latter comprising the largest corps with 2,000 men). Some were Germans, Italians, Poles, or hardened Spanish veterans many of whom had sailed from the Azores. Last but not least were the Mobile Volunteer battalions, some hailing from Porto; others raised in Lisbon, and trained as light troops. The cavalry was also reorganized, units relying heavily on the newly introduced lancer squadrons at the regimental level. Further to this, some contemporary engravings depict Miguelite introducution of lancers, as an experimental unit. The artillery was organized as field batteries relying mostly on 3, 6, and 12 pounders and light howitzers.

On 18 September D. Miguel had Bourmont replaced by Scottish General Macdonell, a veteran with Miguelite command experience in South America. Disgusted by the intrigues of the Miguelite court, Bourmont left for France. With the situation stabilized in Lisbon, Dona Maria II arrived at Tejo from France on 22 September. Meanwhile, on 27 September the Spanish government demanded that D. Miguel expel Don Carlos, the absolutist pretender to the Spanish throne, from Portuguese territory. Miguel ignored this thus raising tensions between Portugal and Spain and abroad. Two days later,

D. Miguel I. (National Library of Portugal)

Fernando VII of Spain died, and his fourth wife Cristina became Queen Regent on behalf of their infant daughter Isabel II. However, the rising of the Carlist movement ensured the path to civil war. The First Carlist War began when the Carlists revolted and proclaimed the Ferdinand VII's brother as King Carlos V of Spain on 5 October. At that moment there were two civil wars raging on the Iberian Peninsula. Both conflicts had similar ideological foundations that would have a serious impact on the foreign policies of Britain and France.

1-11 October 1833: With Saldanha's eastward offensive from Lisbon forcing the Miguelites back to Santarém, the latter strengthened their position whilst harbouring expectations for a change in the management of the war. At that time, France and Britain had recognized the government of Donna Maria II. Politically and militarily weakened, D. Miguel became more isolated. His immediate reaction was to gather the remnants of the army, still a respectable force with a low number of desertions and fanatical units of highly motivated Royalist volunteers. Miguel's strategy was to bring the war to the rural countryside where he had numerous supporters eager to raise guerilla bands. Conversely, Liberal troops primarily hailed from urban centres. Saldanha had to take this into account when planning to campaign in the harsh Portuguese hinterland.

23 October 1833: Following France and England, Belgium also formally recognized the Dona Maria II government.

The Miguelite Army still had claws

2-3 November 1833: Overconfident Liberals launched an a general southward offensive with no more than 1,500 men. Their push pursued pursued part of the Miguelite forces moving from Santarém to the Alentejo. Unfortunately, they underestimated the strength of D. Miguel's forces, still with respectable numbers in infantry, cavalry and artillery. On 2 November, an engagement near Barrosinha village (a short distance from Alcácer do Sal) resulted in a resounding victory for the Miguelites. In fact, to designate the Alcácer action a 'battle' appears somewhat exaggerated. Calling it a large skirmish would be more apropos. Despite this, it was not the disproportionate strength of one side, so much as the quality of equipment and preparations. being brief. The Liberal force largely comprised of an inexperienced and older men troop mix from various contingents. It was also composed of two companies of Englishmen, Alentejo battalion members, a company of French, some cavalry and sailors, making for a total of 1,500 men. In addition to this, the force was poorly equipped in terms of weapons and ammunition. Conversely, the Miguelite force, commanded by General José António de Azevedo Lemos, one of D. Miguel's most important commanders, was well-equipped and composed of veteran troops supported by guerrillas.

Lemos's, Miguelite forces were able to push the Liberals back on to muddy terrain before defeating them. Indeed, a few shots by the Miguelite artillery was enough for Liberal resistance to collapse. This was followed by relentless pursuit to the Sado where desperate Liberals attempted to cross to the far bank in boats. However, a low tide made it impossible to navigate, so most drowned. Others were rounded up on the near bank and and imprisoned in a barn at Alcácer do Sal before being transported to Porto de Rei.

Francisco José de Almeida, an officer in the service of the Liberal army, participated in the action and recollected in *Notes on the Life of an Obscure Man* (1883), the course of events as he experienced them:

Three or four days later, we were ordered to march to Bethlehem, and we went to barracks at the Jeronimos Convent, where I did not linger, so that at eleven o'clock I marched with a detachment of two captains to Belém Tower, where the brave baron of Pico de Celeiro was governor of the old fortress.

We did campaign work there, and after a few days the detachment was ordered to march to Setubal, which we did by boarding in the Navy Arsenal at five o'clock in the afternoon and arriving at Moita, where we arrived at midnight.

At dawn we marched to Setubal, where we arrived at three o'clock in the afternoon. Mr. Lieutenant João Augusto Marques and I went to the house of a Genoese, whose name was José Estrafaz, who had a liquor store. Our host was a brazen Miguelite and, as someone told us, he had offered free of charge the precise wood for the gallows that had risen there and had a stage where he could see the executions more quietly! I think we will therefore have an idea of how badly we would be received and treated by our host ... From Setúbal we marched, embarked, to Alcácer and we disembarked to the beach. The enemy, as we approached, retreated and we entered Alcácer, a land where everyone was constitutional and who welcomed us with frankness and joy. The bells tolled, and the village, despite the copious rain falling ... Lieutenant Marques and I were settled at the house of a fellow named Silva, receiving us, both he and his good family, in a way that still arouses gratitude, not only for his generous frankness but also for another reason, who was interested in me when I was later taken prisoner. We kept ourselves in Alcácer with no event worth noting, except a few artillery pieces sent to us and in such a state that they never left the place where they landed, until, finally, the wretched November 2, 1833, when, after the discovery (of the approaching of the Miguelite troops), marched the force of which I was part to a place called Port of Lama and another part of the force to a place on the left, whose name I do not remember now ... our commander, Colonel Florencio, had been warned that the enemy attacked us that day, as it did attack us.

We must now say something about the organization of the force that was sent to Alcácer because, as it was unfortunate, it is necessary to seek to know the truth in order to do justice.

The force seems to me to be 1500 soldiers, made up of contingents taken from the seven fixed corps of Lisbon, which were so named because they were made up of older and less fierce people, from two companies of English soldiers, from the Battalion of Alentejo, from a company of French, some sailors and soldiers of the former navy brigade, of twenty-three cavalry troopers of the 11th Regiment and a force of the 4th mobile battalion, of which I was part, as well as Lieutenant Marques, Lieutenant Facadas (from Évora) and Brevet Major Assis, who was our commander, and Captain Morais. It is quite clear that the elements of which the force was composed were as heterogeneous as possible, which is always detrimental to the good outcome of an action. In addition, his state of ammunition was terrible, so I noted the strength of my battalion, as it had little gunpowder and still had the same flints on the weapons with which it had made fire on September 5th, and I was told that the other contingents were no better off. This was, as I now remember, a little more or less the state of the force, and this is its organization when it marched to meet the enemy. I must say that having been taken prisoner and losing my luggage, I lost my notes. Therefore, some inaccuracy is committed to this in what I say. Arriving at the point where we should wait for the enemy, we took a position on a small hill, on top of which was a thing called fort [sic]. The terrain was sandy and the lack of land and stone made such construction uneven. There was a small artillery piece there, and they gave me twelve brigade soldiers and one sergeant, who knew nothing of artillery, and fourteen soldiers of my battalion for garrison. The rest of the force retreated to the rear to stand in the nearby pine forest. As soon as I took office, it was my first care to examine the cannon and its ammunition. Unfortunately, I was extremely surprised to see that the wheels of the piece were broken, that there were no fuses or die, that there were only nine solid shots, eight cartridges and a small half-barrel of loose powder. I immediately went to look for Colonel Florencio, and in particular I gave him part of what he had found, to which he answered me a little sharply: «Yes! Go there That the necessary measures will already be taken!

I went back to my place and had a small fire lit, where I kept sticks lit to serve as a port fires. From the loose gunpowder I had some of it moistened and made a few "kneaded" pyramids to serve instead of a fuse, and I had the piece loaded, hoping for my luck. It was an hour or so in the afternoon when this happened. Shortly afterwards, a soldier of the Baleizão militias turned out to have deserted from the enemy and gave exact news of his approach. I had compassion of his state and presentation - a subscription was made for his dressing among people present and I shared with him a good lunch that my good hosts were sending to Lieutenant Marques, me and my comrades. It would be a couple of hours, the enemy passed in front of me, in a place called Cortiças and put their artillery in a ditch, a little to the left, making it into us a terrible and well-sustained fire, so his artillery was very well served. and, at the second shot, a bullet killed the navy brigade officer who was a commander, and I think captain. This official came for me to talk about when it was hit by the bullet it killed. As we can, the eight shots were fired corresponding to the eight cartridges that were placed; but unfortunately I was, at this interval, injured in the left leg by a shrapnel, that left me immobilized for some time. Fortunately, my sergeant, who calls Paulo Jorge, was a stout and brave man, so he continued to make fire with a piece such as. Musketry did not occur because it was not seen who to shoot. Becoming better, I returned to my post and saw that I had no more ammunition left to continue to make use of the useless piece to remain there. As a result, I jammed the artillery piece with the remaining bullet and I withdraw by heading to the pine forest, where to find the troops. Unfortunately, they had already withdrawn. I then followed my people along the road leading to Alcácer, which is flanked on the right by the river and (current season) on the left for a ditch. On the road I met two English companies, which were run by two officers, which, it seems to me, were called Bailey and another Fitzpatrick. I joined them with the accompanying soldiers, and that assembled force resisted an enemy cavalry squadron that was pursued us up to the village square. There our brave English captain, seeing that it was impossible to resist for missing or holding flanks, I do not know what order he gave. What I know about everyone disbanded, and I got in a small road leading to the river, and when I got there, I saw a lot of disorder and people wanting to cross the river, it was almost impossible due to the low tide and the boats in dry docks. Unfortunately, those who tried to pass the sludge got drowned in the mud. What happened on the left I don't know; It is probable that the officer, Lieutenant Reis, who was reported to me in charge of a artillery gun similar to mine, which was posted there, was no happier than I am with ammunition. However, I believe that, despite this, it has fulfilled its duty. From the state in which I saw things, I recognized that we were lost and, worse, that we had been cut. Under such circumstances, I walked as I could to where there was a dock and a tent. I asked the people who were there to charity me to see if I could escape being taken prisoner and even shot by the fire that the enemy was making to the fugitives. Unfortunately, these people repelled me, and shortly afterwards two guerrillas and a cavalry soldier on foot took me prisoner, who, without mistreating me, took me to a high place, where was the commander of the enemy force, the famous General Lemos. When I arrived, I saw prisoners there too, the two English officers, my major Assis, Captain Manuel José Gomes, the captain of Morais Caçadores who were attached to my battalion, my two sergeants Paulo Jorge and Ferro, D. Joaquim (Count of Penafiel's brother),

Mr. Pachecos (from Setúbal), many soldiers from my battalion and other corps, many English, etc., which in all were four hundred and thirty-two men. Immediately afterwards came to me a prisoner, naked and badly treated, the unfortunate Carlos Cavigioli. After a while they brought me and the two English officers to General Lemos, who was at a distance on horseback in a blue frock coat and oiled cocked hat. He asked the English if they wanted to be of service to D. Miguel, to which the brave officers answered no. Coming to me mr. Bailey said to me, "Never!"

Then he called me and asked me: "Do you want to be of service?" I say no, and that I would suffer the fate of my comrades with resignation. To this answered the general, smiling: "Get him that band and that sword ... that will follow the fate of his comrades!" After that an officer came to me and gave me a tremendous slap, saying: "Very great rogue, who was caught with his mouth in the cylinder!"

Then the soldiers took off my band and sword, stripped me of my frock coat and trousers, leaving me only in long johns and shirt! And because I had two gold rings on one finger and they couldn't take them off, due to the work with the artillery gun and agitation I had that day had made my finger thicken, they wanted to cut it! Luckily the rings came out, and I was completely robbed! I apologize for telling these things carefully, because while I do not want to comment on the behaviour of the late general, who can no longer defend himself, I want to know that there was a man, who called himself a gentleman – a general, a military man, a Portuguese! – that he allowed to be practiced in his presence in the person of a prisoner, a Portuguese who had loyally fought, which I have just faithfully told you! I am relieved to interrupt the story of the unfortunate prisoners with this rambling that concerns only me.

Gathering the prisoners, he sent me a cavalry officer to take charge of my comrades and command them to the village. I replied that I could not command them, since there were some among them with rank higher than mine. The result of this just observation of mine was that the official said to rage at me and shout at me: "Do what I tell you or put this sword in your mouth."

Then I turned to my wretched fellows and said to them: "You see, I'm obliged!" To which all replied: "Come on! Come on!" In view of this, he said: "I ask you to get in order, and we march to the village." No sooner said than done. We went to the jail door where they divided us. Then they got us into various houses, so there was no prison where we could all fit. So a large portion of the prisoners were put in a barn, of which I was a part, as well as the Mr. Pachecos.

I must declare, to be fair, that the officer who commanded the force that escorted us to the village behaved with dignity and did not allow them to harm us. That gentleman talked to me and told me he was from Bragança, and I told him that he also had my aunts and other relatives, whom I named him, whom he said he knew very well. I learned later that when he returned to Bragança, he had told my aunts of me. I am sorry I do not know the name of such a worthy military man, to write it here with gratitude, and I would greatly appreciate that he still lived, to see that I do him justice.

When I separated the officers, the unfortunate sergeant Paulo Jorge asked me to give him as an officer, because he took care of him, the officers would always be better treated, and I unfortunately agreed to his request, and, with this consent, unintentionally killed him! Poor man who belonged to a family of gentlemen, of good men, and so he thought that his murderers would think as men who honor themselves and humans honour themselves ... [7]

---

7 Francisco José de Almeida was an Ensign in Liberal Army, and already an old man published, in 1883, his memories, mostly from his youth in the Civil War, untitled *Notas da Vida de um Homem Obscuro* or *Notes on the Life of an*

It is said that in this battle the Liberal army lost more men than during the entire war. This may or may not be true. Absence of corroborating evidence and attempts by Liberal historians to minimize losses causes one to consider the claim with extreme caution.

Also associated with this battle is the execution of 26 Liberal officers of General Francisco de Paula Botelho de Moraes Sarmento's command. Imprisoned by the victorious Miguelites, the lax military code of the time determined that officers defecting from the Portuguese Army to make war on rebel forces were under sentence of death if convicted. Moreover, the Miguelites were out for revenge for a previous massacre of their officers at Panóias on 14 August 1833. Thus the 26 unfortunate officers were shot by firing squad two days after the battle. The atrocity would come to be known as the 'Algalé massacre'. This episode was but one crude example of the deep hatred between the opposing factions.

The defeat was a serious warning for D. Pedro and Saldanha inasmuch that the Miguelite Army still retained a capacity for campaigning if not faced by superior numbers. In addition, the war had changed from siege operations to a conflict of open battles. Both sides still employed British fighting doctrine of Peninsular War vintage. Unfortunately, the level of training and discipline required for this was beyond the mostly untrained troops. This was especially true on the Liberal side which relied on the Mobile Volunteer battalions and line regiment recruits Furthermore, trained foreign troops were spread too thin to impact combat efficiency and readiness.

Although suffering a major setback at the Siege of Porto, the Miguelite Army still had many veterans within its ranks. These men had experience of the Beresford reorganization of the Portuguese Army in 1810, so general proficiency with the legendary musket volley fire procedure was fairly widespread. The Miguelites also possessed well-trained artillerymen to crew their gun arsenal. For their part, the Royalist volunteers excelled at irregular operations. Any lack of fighting skills was made up for by a fanatical devotion to the Miguelite cause. If inefficient with siege warfare, the Miguelites were far more skillful in open field operations, the bane of D. Pedro's urban raised troops. Thus the Miguelite way of war was in need of serious re-evaluation by the Liberals if they were to defeat their opponents. The towns and villages of the Portuguese hinterland were still under D. Miguel's control. Matters were made worse when the conflict spread across the Portuguese-Spanish border. In early 1834, Spanish General Rodil dispatched troops into Portugal to defeat D. Carlos and his supporters. Rodil was ultimately unsuccessful, but forced his quarry to flee in an attempt to reach D. Miguel's friendly forces.

Liberals and Miguelites Clash in Ribatejo

14-16 January 1834: In order to secure Portugal's central regions during the winter of 1834, 4,500 Liberals under personal command of Marshal Saldanha attacked Leiria from two sides in an attempt to encircle the Miguelite forces there. In order to avoid this, the Miguelites, abandoned Leiria Castle to seek refuge in Coimbra. Saldanha, prior to ordering a pursuit, strengthened Leiria's defences as a precaution against a possible combined Miguelite and Carlist counterattack. He was also aware that his force was not large enough to control central Portugal.

30 January-2 February 1834: In the vicinity of Pernes, near Santarém, there were two successive engagements. The first, the Action at Pernes, occurred on 11 November 1833 between Saldanha's force and the Miguelites defending the Ribeira de Pernes mill from where D. Miguel's troops, in Almeirim, were

---

Obscure Man (translated title). This quite long transcription translated to English by the author from the original Portuguese gives us a colourful description of combat and consequences of a civil war.

supplied with flour. Achieving surprise, Saldanha's force defeated the small mill garrison before destroying the facilities there. It was at Pernes where the most important of the two engagements, in this case a full-scale battle, took place on 30 January 1834. The situation for the Liberal Army could be critical for the rest of the country in that the best troops were with with Saldanha at Pernes. Saldanha was well aware of the Alcácer do Sal reverse, so could not spare reinforcements. Nevertheless, he carried all before him with the trifling loss of 10 killed or wounded. Numerous prisoners and several battle flags were seized. Field Marshal Pedro António Machado Pinto de Sousa Canavarro's force suffered some 900 casualties, mostly drowned in the Alviela, whilst attempting to flee the Liberal light infantry and cavalry.

18 February 1834: On 18 February 1834, General Álvaro Xavier da Fonseca Coutinho e Póvoas led his army to Asseca bridge near Almoster. It controlled the roads to Lisbon through Santarém, the main base for D. Miguel's army. Miguelite dominance did not only exist in this region. Indeed, despite a number of Liberal victories in the provinces of Trás-os-Montes, Minho and Beira Alta where D. Miguel followers, many of which served with the volunteers and in guerrilla bands, still dominated.

Marshal Saldanha, commander of the Liberal forces, planned, whilst maintaining the siege of Santarém, to attack with a part of his force, the cities of Leiria and Coimbra. This would isolate the Miguelite defenders of Santarém from central province reinforcements. Saldanha's troops gathered at Rio Maior with troops dispatched from Lisbon. On 16 January, Leiria was assaulted from two sides. Finding themselves almost cut off, the Miguelites abandoned Leiria Castle for refuge in Coimbra. Following this, in early February, General Póvoas, commander of the Miguelite troops, devised a plan to attack the Liberals at Pernes and Santarém to relieve the pressure on his forces. Alert to the possibility of such an offensive, Saldanha took the necessary precautions in anticipation of the enemy's next move. Póvoas, facing the growing Liberal power, concocted a new plan, which was an assault on Ponte de Asseca as a means of clearing the way to Lisbon where a Miguelite counter-revolution was expected to break out. Dividing his force in two on 18 February, Póvoas marched over the Asseca with approximately 4,000 troops without launching a full-scale attack because this was not the core part of the plan. For his part, Póvoas did not want to risk his force whilst traversing rough terrain against the veteran Saldanha. His presence was a morale boost to the Liberal army. Póvoas's primary aim was a diversion manoeuvre to divide the Liberal lines. Meantime, the Miguelite Commander-in-chief General José António de Azevedo Lemos, advanced with some 4,500-5,000 men towards Almoster and Santa Maria before breaching the Liberal lines, the latter presumably attempting to repel Póvoas's attack. Forced to extend and thereby weakening, his defensive lines, Saldanha gained the advantage, as the terrain his men occupied formed a narrow canyon between overgrown and dense hills.

Saldanha would later be credited for having understood Lemos's intentions and reversed the situation by setting a trap. The claim the he allegedly allowed the Miguelites to climb the gorge once the Santa Maria bridge was traversed lack foundation. Accounts of the battle by contemporary historians and former officers in the Liberal Army (Simão José da Luz Soriano and Baron of Saint Pardoux do not support this theory. According to Soriano,[8] the Liberals appear to have merely followed Miguelite movements, hastily reacting to them whilst they occurred. Saldanha, indecisive during that time, was vexed by the possibility of a concentration of 10,000 Miguelites storming the Almoster line despite the problematic terrain. Charging in columns with beating drums under heavy enemy fire, the Miguelite infantry pressed on with great bravery despite appalling casualties. Miguelite commanders General Santa Clara and Brigadier Brassaget,

8 Simão José da Luz Soriano, *História da Guerra Civil.* Tomes. I to VI (Lisboa: Imprensa Nacional, 1887), Tome V, pp. 219-23.

who promptly replaced the former at the front of his men, were killed. The battle remained undecided until, "on his own initiative", according to Luz Soriano, the Liberal Colonel Queirós with his crack 2nd and 12th Caçadores battalions, rushed the Miguelite flank in order to prevent a retreat to Santa Maria bridge whilst the 3rd and 6th line infantry regiments, command by Brigadier Brito, charged the Miguelites at bayonet point.[9] Placing himself in harm's way. Saldanha personally led the 1st Infantry Regiment (the same regiment which he had manoeuvred with remarkable skill during the famous Battle of Bussaco in 1810).

Only then did D. Miguel's troops understand the terrible situation they were in. Seeing his infantry in danger of being massacred, General Lemos ordered his cavalry to engage the Liberal forces, but Brigadier Bacon, at the head of Queen's Lancer veterans, charged with the usual shock effect, The consequent Miguelite losses exceeded a 1,000 men. However, the way in which they withdrew was, from a military standpoint, impeccable. Thus further casualties were prevented. The Liberals also sustained significant casualties thus demonstrating that Miguel's troops were a force to be reckoned with. This was a warning to the Liberal high command to engage battle-hardened Portuguese and foreign troops as opposed to volunteers and raw recruits. They should rely on the veterans, both Portuguese and foreigners to take major offensives against the Miguelite army.[10]

Battle of Almoster 18 February 1834. (Author's collection)

9 Soriano, *História da Guerra Civil.*, p. 221.
10 Soriano, *História da Guerra Civil.*, p. 223.

10 March 1834: On the Alentejo front, the town of Serpa was besieged by the Belgian troops. To the north, Liberal troops advanced from Porto and regained control of Minho province, which was situated near the the Spanish border.

Northern Front

18 March 1834: New offensives, commanded by Admiral Napier, were launched on land and sea in Minho province. On 23 March, the fortress and town of Caminha was seized. This resulted in Liberal control of Minho river. On 27 March, Colonel Sebastião Cabreira occupied Santo Tirso near Porto. This opened the way to Braga, which was occupied on 2 April. The following day, Liberal forces under the command of the Duke of Terceira entered the enormous fortress of Valença do Minho. Northern Portugal was now secured. The Liberals could now focus on the conquest of the centre provinces where there was a strong Miguelite presence. Following his capture of Valença, the Duke of Terceira led a full-scale expedition to the centre and occupied Viseu, Coimbra and Tomar. Despite their large number of sympathizers, D. Miguel's army, under the command of General Guedes, suffered from lack of ammunition and food, retreated east in the face of D. Pedro's advancing forces. Bollaert provided a vivid account of the miltary operations at this time:

> This was a smart soldiering affair, and rather on his own account. He was evidently fond of army strategy and tactics. He delighted in scaling forts, and other suchlike operations. On the 23rd of March Napier communicated to D. Pedro: " I have taken the castle and town of Caminha, and I am marching on Vianna." He followed up his success, and threatened the governor of Valença, that if he did not surrender in two hours he would bring up his " battery train." He had not a gun. The "train" was but a name, the name he bore, and that won Valença. On the 3rd of April he received the keys of a fortress so well garrisoned and bristling with artillery, that it ought to have required 7000 to 8000 men, with heavy artillery, to have invested it, at least pro forma.

Bollaert also went on record that:

> Whilst we in the flotilla were guarding the river, Admiral Napier went with a squadron and troops to the north in March. We heard the following of the Admiral's campaign – The Spanish governor of Vigo invited Napier and his principal officers to a dinner. The main object at this dinner was to pass the wine freely, and when the governor was in good humour, to ask his permission to land a few men at Vigo; at his consent, certain officers were to retire and proceed on board, the men comprising the expedition being in the boats awaiting orders. They were to land, and march in all haste to the River Minho, the frontier line. All this followed without loss of time. Napier put himself at their head, making direct for the ferry leading over the river Minho to Caminha. He so timed his march as to arrive on the opposite bank at nightfall, when all the boats were quietly taken possession of at the ferry, and a number of men sent over to surprise and capture the picket, if possible without firing a shot. All these movements were easily accomplished, as no enemy was expected to cross over from Spain. The countersign was extorted by threats. All the force was now brought over on Portuguese ground, a strong guard was sent to the entrance of this walled town; the correct countersign being given, the gates were opened, and the guard, taken by surprise, wore secured without the firing of a shot.

Napier entered the fortress with his entire force. Making for the main arsenal, opposite to which was the governor's house, the governor, on hearing the unusual tramping of men, rushed out onto the balcony followed by his aide-de-camp. Discerning marine red coats, he called out "Miguelistas! Às armas!" ("Miguelites! to Arms!"). A resultant musket volley cut down the governor and his aide, the only two lives lost during the seizure of the fortified town. On reaching the arsenal, the were arms were secured in racks. The British cutter yacht, *Scorpion*, laden with small arms for D. Miguel,and commanded by Lieutenant Whitaker, ex-R.N, and a private contractor which had arrived the day before from England, became a prize. Town after town, some fortified, surrendered to Napier 'by letter' as he termed it. With a flag of truce, he dispatched letters to several governors, demanding surrender within 24 hours, informing them this was only the advance guard of a larger force. The governors knew of the Miguelite retreat from Porto and from Lisbon on Santarém. Napier had conquered the north coast, the Duke of Terceira and General Torres were successfully campaigning in the north-east; Baron of Sá da Bandeira, Bernardo de Sá Nogueira was in the south campaigning in the Algarves and Saldanha confronted D. Miguel before Santarém. D. Pedro left Lisbon for Cartaxo on 9 April, but returned in bad health and spirits. Saldanha pressing him on the one hand to dismiss ministers, and, on the other hand, the ministers pleaded to retain their posts.

On 25 March, the celebrated defender of Serra Convent, the now General Torres, marched out of Oporto with the greater part of the garrison. Torres dispatched a column to Braga, on the approach of which the Miguelite Governor Raimundo Joze Pinheiro fled to Carvalho d'Este with his battalion of volunteer monks, two pieces of artillery and some cavalry. The Liberals, however, had to pursue Pinheiro in order to clear the area. Torres now had to deal with General Joze Cardozo's advanced posts at Santo Tirso, driving them out. On 2 April, he found Cardozo positioned on the heights of Lixa, after which he charged. Swept from the field, Cardozo's force sustained 112 casualties, many of which were wounded, and lost two field guns. Torres lost 12 officers and 88 men.

Having crossed Tamega, the Liberals again confronted Cardozo at the Amarante bridge. The Miguelities were established in a strong position. Here Torres received orders to hand over command to Terceira, who had disembarked with a battalion of 12th Caçadores at Porto 3 April. On 11 April, at daybreak, a part of Terceira's force passed over the Tamega under Colonel Queiróz command. Another force crossed the bridge supported by artillery and, charging the, dislodged them. The Liberals, having gained the Mesão Frio heights lost 3 killed and a handful of wounded. The Miguelites lost 20 dead on, some wounded and 100 prisoners. Two artillery pieces with plenty of ammunition were also captured. Terceira pursued by the road to Régua in Trás-os-Montes province, but the Miguelites managed to flee to Vila Real. The Duke, however, overtook them at Castro d'Aire and defeated them on 30 April. The Miguelites sustained numerous killed and wounded, and 120 prisoners. The remainder of their force fled via the Viseu road to Coimbra, which the Duke da Terceira entered on 8 May. On 16 April, Torres attacked the Miguelites near the Douro, driving them into Coimbra, after which he returned to Porto.

On the international scene, 22 April 1834, the Quadruple Alliance was signed in opposition to the Holy Alliance. Portugal, Spain, Great Britain, and France agreed to banish D. Miguel from Portugal and D. Carlos from Spain. Britain promised naval support for D. Pedro and Isabel of Spain, and Portugal agreed to supply an auxiliary force for operations against D. Carlos. This force became the Portuguese Auxiliary Division iduring the First Carlist War.

Battle of Asseiceira and War's End

16 May 1834: The Duke of Terceira's forces were joined by Colonel Vasconcellos on 14 May. That evening, Terceira occupied Tomar, the enemy having withdrawn on his approach. On 15 May, he communicated with Marshal Saldanha all that he knew of the enemy's position and intentions. During the course of the day, an intercepted letter from General Guedes stated his force was encamped in the neighbourhood of Asseiceira. In it he ordered the artillery coming from Santarém to halt at Golegã. This led the Duke to suppose it was Guedes's intention to withdraw from his position. Determined to prevent this either by bringing him to action the following day or following up a retirement, Terceira, on the night of 15/16 May, attacked the Miguelite Army camped in a strong position on the Asseiceira heights, a system of hills and valleys about 6.5 km from Tomar. D. Miguel himself was at Santarém and was not involved in the ensuing battle. Terceira, advanced from Tomar on the morning of 16 May and attacked the Miguelite position in three columns commanded by Colonels Queiróz, Nepomuceno and Vasconcellos, the cavalry commanded by Colonel Fonseca. The Miguelite's attempted to repel them with artillery and cavalry. Nevertheless, the Liberal forces persisted, and with a decisive cavalry assault, carried the heights.

Terceira, in combined movement with Saldanha and General Rodil, met the enemy on the Asseiceira heights which are approximately 25 km north of Santarém. The Miguelites were commanded by General Guedes. His force, consisting of retreating troops of the northern division and strong reinforcements from Santarém, sent by D. Miguel, amounted to some 6,000 men. Terceira divided his force into the three columns The attack was impetuous, with massive infantry assaults screened by Caçadores, Fonseca's cavalry anticipating a chance to turn the Miguelite flanks. The Miguelite defence was worthy of desperate men struggling to preserve a lost cause. According to Bollaert:

> A moment of anxiety pervaded the Queen's troops, but the Duke ordered a charge of cavalry at a critical moment, and confusion dispersed the bravo Miguelite band, to fight no more battles for their master.

On the morning of 16 May, the Liberals marched from Tomar via the Atalaia road, and soon discovered the Miguelites massed on the Asseiceira heights some 7 km from Tomar. Colonel Queiróz advanced on the right, Nepomuceno in the centre, and Vasconcellos on the left. Guedes forces were defeated at Asseiceira. Three colonels, several lieutenant-colonels and majors were amongst the 64 officers taken prisoner. Eight pieces of light artillery also fell into the Duke's hands. The Queen's troops lost 22 officers and 266 men. The evacuation of Santarém was decided upon, and the Miguelites retreated towards Évora. The enemy, favoured by strong defensive positions and artillery, made a vigorous resistance, made a determined stand with repeated cavalry charges with at every favourable opportunity. Repulsed by the right and centre columns, closely formed, with 'great gallantry' (Bollaert), proving by their firmness that they would not be broken or prevented from gaining the heights. The Miguelite counter-attacks having been blunted, they were obliged to withdraw via the Punhete and Torres Vedras roads into the adjacent mountains and valleys closely pursued by the Queen's infantry and cavalry. A decided charge by the latter put the enemy's squadrons to flight, killing and wounding a considerable number, and taking 1,400 prisoners, including 74 officers, 4 battle flags, and all of the enemy's artillery (8 field guns, mainly 6 pounders).

On the 17th, Terceira was at Golegã, Napier occupied Torres Novas, and D. Pedro advanced at once to Santarém. Retiring across the Tagus towards the Alentejo, the Miguelites evacuated Santarém that day. Marshal Saldanha immediately occupying the latter place. Thereafter, Terceira and Saldanha, crossing the Tagus at different points, were instructed to follow up the enemy whilst bestowing amnesty to those willing to lay down their arms. This also applied to D. Miguel on condition that he quit the Peninsula for good.

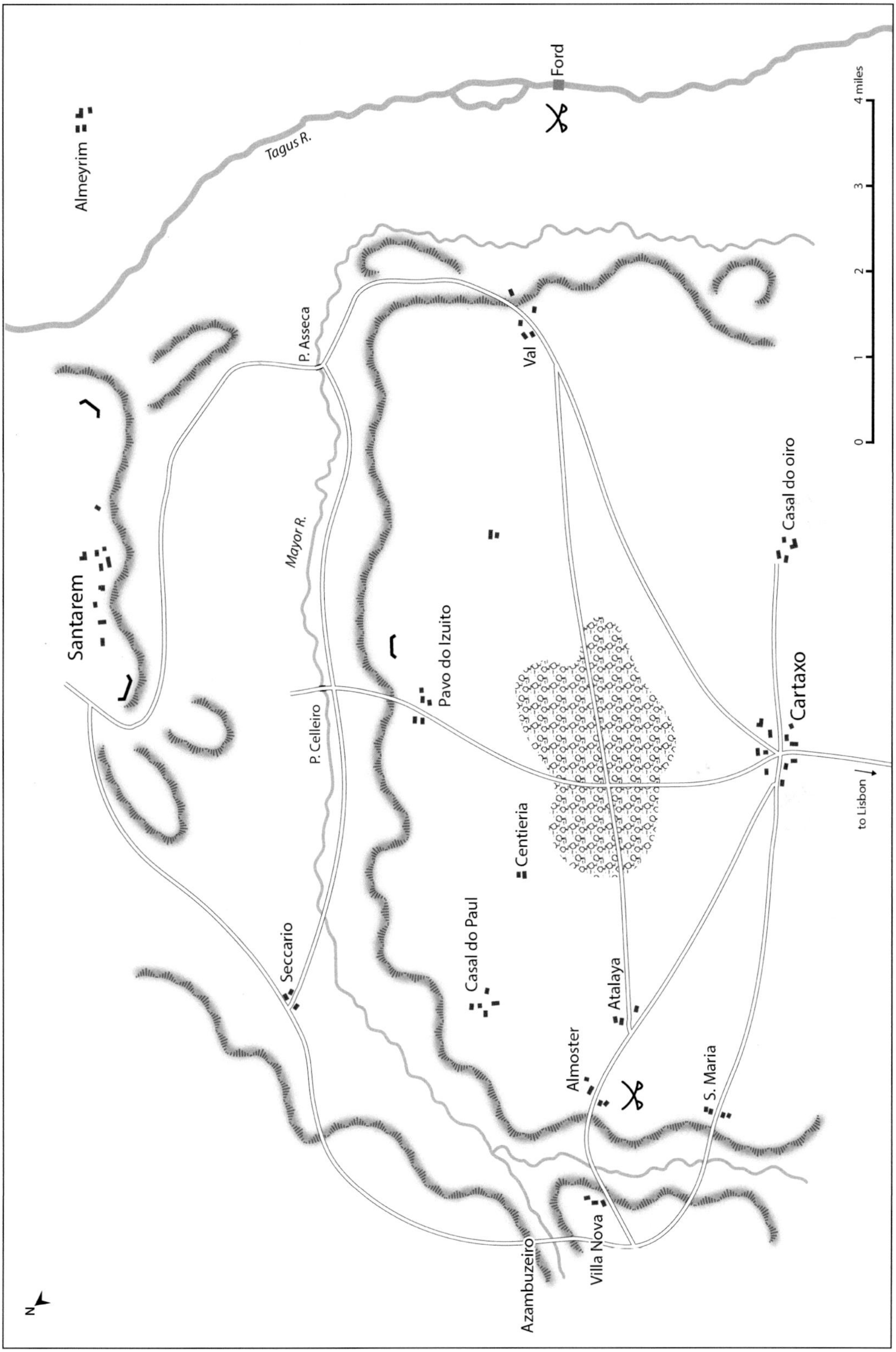

Position of Donna Maria's Army before Santarem 1834.

The Miguelites, thus surrounded, and their retreat to Spain cut off by the new Liberal government of that country, halted in Évora Monte. D. Miguel still had a respectable army of some 18,000 men, but no artillery ammunition supply. Facing the Liberal 'iron ring', the Miguelite forces sullenly accepted the terms granted by the Convention of Évora Monte (26 May 1834). By consensual agreement of the Liberal high command, the surrender terms were not harsh. D. Pedro, in the name of his daughter, Queen Dona Maria II, had decreed clemency and pardon for all. D. Miguel was banished forever.

27 May 1834: Despite some 18,000 men still in the ranks D. Miguel's officers were unwilling to risk a final battle after nearly two years of continuous warfare. Thus D. Miguel was induced to capitulate and renounce all claims to the Portuguese throne before going into exile.

1 June 1834: Both D. Miguel and D. Carlos departed Portugal from Sines on the British Frigate *Stag*. Miguel ended up in Austria via Italy never to return. Carlos returned to Spain via Britain. On 20 June 1834, in Genoa, prior to travelling to Vienna, D. Miguel renounced the Monte Évora Convention, but never returned to Portugal. He died in the Austrian capitol in 1866.

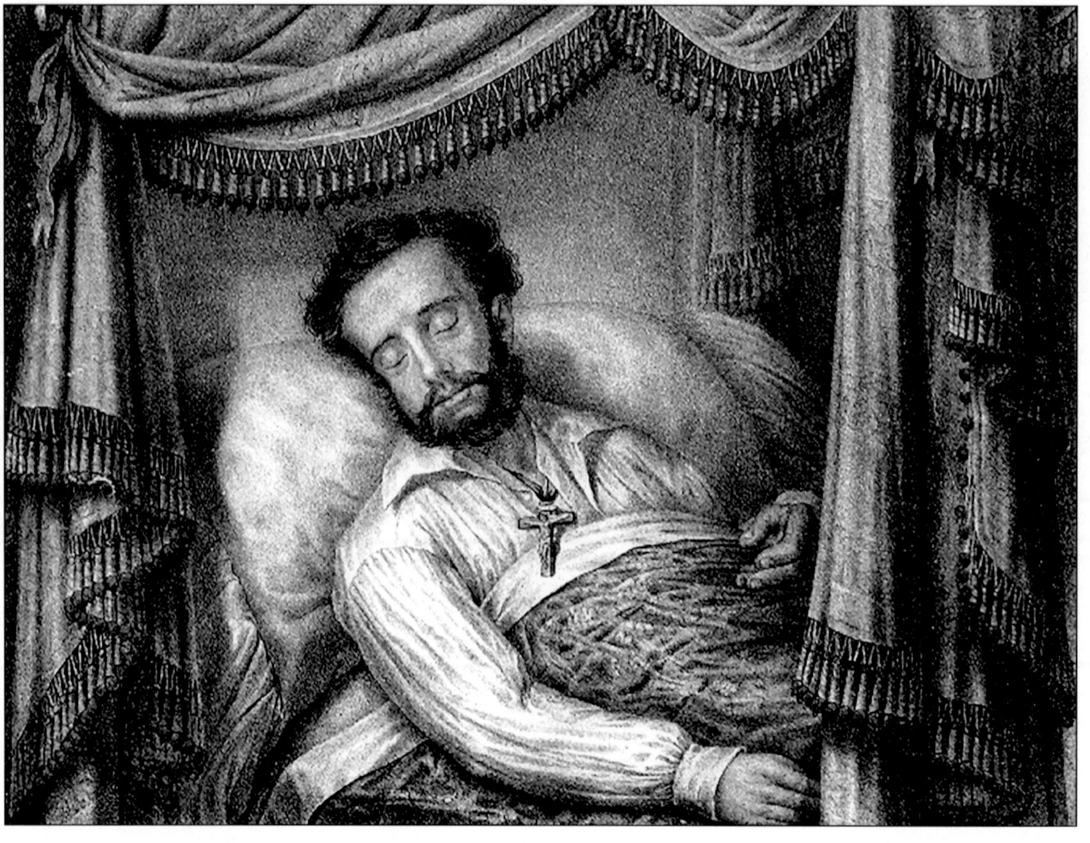

Death of D. Pedro by Dias da Costa. (Casa da Marquesa de Santos, Rio de Janeiro)

20 September 1834: Finally, after 6 years of open conflict, Queen D. Maria II swore to uphold the Constitutional Charter of 1826. Four days later, on 24 September 1834, D. Pedro died of tuberculosis. The various Liberal parties never forgave him for pardoning Miguel. One of Pedro's greatest humiliations occurred during a state visit to Porto that same year. It was whilst attending a performance at the Royal Theatre that the audience, recollecting the long and bloody siege, booed the Duke of Bragança for his leniency towards the hated Miguelites.

Aftermath

D. Pedro was very ill with tuberculosis and, following his triumph, had increasing difficulties in holding the political and military factions together. Left unpaid, unfed and without supplies, the foreign troops were shamefully neglected, their British officers leaving in disgust. Shaw vainly attempted to obtain the promised pay for his valiant Scots. Free passage home was also promised. Swearing continued loyalty to D. Miguel' cause, the Scotsmen were forced on board at gunpoint. Not one received the promised parcel of land. Few if any of the officers got anything at all and it took years for many of them to obtain a proportion of the money due and some were never paid. Curiously, it was the despised Sir John Milley Doyle who was instrumental in having the claims partially settled with the appointment of an Anglo-Portuguese Commission. In retribution, the Portuguese never paid Doyle who, left penniless, died a Military Knight

Queen Dona Maria II. (National Library of Portugal)

of Windsor. D. Pedro might have done more for the gallant foreigners. He recognized how much Portugal owed them before dying on 24 September 1834 at the age of 35. His integrity, honesty and leadership would be sadly missed.

Tragically, Portugal was to lurch from crisis to crisis over the next few years, a second civil war and another siege of Porto breaking out in 1846. No foreign participation (except for Ronald Macdonell who returned to head the reactionaries. occurred this time. He died at the head of a reconnaissance mission. Many British veterans went on to serve with Sir George de Lacy Evans's 'British Legion' during the Carlist War. They went on to encounter the same incompetence, neglect and ingratitude. Shaw joined the Legion, fighting well as usual, before resigning in disgust. Hodges was knighted and went on to serve as British consul to Serbia, Alexandria, and Hamburg. He maintained a steady correspondence with Napier, meeting him on more than one occasion when opportunity provided. Napier re-entered the Royal Navy and served with distinction and some controversy. It was he who led a British fleet into the Baltic during the Crimean War (1853-56). Napier did well there despite some criticism, but retired under a cloud. A man always in need of a challenge, Shaw became Chief Commissioner of the Manchester Police.

Unusually, for a conflict prior to 1870, let alone a conflict like the Portuguese Civil War of 1832-34, there are existent literate voices from the ranks – Waterloo veteran Corporal Thomas Knight and 16-year-old private Alexander Tolmer. Both searched for adventure and found it in the elite Queen's Lancers. There are also a number of other memoirs, mostly serving officers who filled a contemporary demand for personal accounts. Napier, Shaw, Hodges and Glascock also provided admirable personal accounts. All are evocative of The War of the Two Brothers.

Bibliography

Archival Sources

Chronica Constitucional do Porto. July-December (Porto: Typographia Gandra e Filhos, 1832).
Chronica Constitucional do Porto. January-December (Porto: Typographia Gandra e Filhos, 1833).
Chronica Constitucional de Lisboa. July-December (Lisboa: ed, Imprensa Nacional, 1833).
Noticia Official das Operações do Exército Libertador. July to September (Porto: Typographia Gandra e Filhos, 1833).
Lista Geral dos Officiaes do Exército Libertador referida ao dia 25 de Julho de 1833. (Lisbon: ed. Typographia de A.J.C. Cruz, 1835).
Ordens do Dia do Exército de D. Miguel. January to December (n.ed. Porto,1832).
Ordens do Dia do Exército de D. Miguel. January to August (n.ed. Porto,1833).
Ordens do Dia do Exército de D. Pedro. October 1828 to November 1832 (Porto: Typographia Gandra e Filhos, 1832).
Ordens do Dia do Exército de D. Pedro. November 1832 to August 1833 (Porto: Typographia Gandra e Filhos, 1833).

Published Sources

Alexander, J. E., *Sketches in Portugal during the civil war of 1834* (London: James Cochrane and Co., 1835).
Anon., *Esclarecimentos sobre a Guerra Civil de Portugal, o sítio do Porto, e a morte de S.M. Imperial O Senhor D. Pedro, Duque de Bragança de saudosa memória, escriptos por um estrangeiro* (Lisbon: ed. Galhardo & Irmãos, 1836).
Anon., *Campagne de six mois dans le Royaume des Algarves et Portugal* (Brussels: J. de Mat, Imprimeur-Libraire, 1834).
Anon., *Journal d'un officier français au service de Don Miguel pendant les campagnes de Portugal en 1833 et 1834.* (Paris: Chez G.A. Denton, Imprimeur-Libraire, 1834).
Anon., *Manifesto de sua Majestade Fidellissima El Rei Nosso Senhor o Senhor D. Miguel I* (Lisbon: Impressão Régia, 1832).
Anon., *Revista Histórica de Portugal, desde a morte de D. João VI até o falecimento do Imperador D. Pedro* (Porto: ed. Typographia Commercial, 1846).
Badcock, L., *Rough leaves from a Journal kept in Spain and Portugal, during the years 1832, 1833 and 1834* (London: ed. Richard Bentley, New Burlington Street, 1835).
Bollaert. W., *Wars of Succession of Portugal and Spain from 1826 to 1840 with resume of the political History of Portugal and Spain to the presente time.* Vol. I (London: Charing Cross, 1870).
Historia abreviada do Cerco da cidade do Porto durante os annos de 1832 (Lisboa: Jornal do Exercito Portuguez, 1841).

Historia do Cerco do Porto: a guerra civil, o Sítio do Porto até à morte de D. Pedro IV (Porto: Typ. Empreza Popular, 1870).

Historia da Restauração de Portugal por S.M.I o Duque de Bragança contendo a relação de batalhas e victorias do exercito constitucional (Rio de Janeiro: Typographia de Laemmert, 1841).

Hodges. G.L., *Narrative of the expedition to Portugal in 1832, under the orders of His Imperial Majesty D. Pedro, duke of Braganza* (London: James Fraser, 1833).

Mins, P., *A Narrative of the Naval part of the Expedition to Portugal under the orders of His Imperial Majesty Dom Pedro Duke of Braganza* (London: ed. Sherwood, Gilbert & Piper, 1833).

Napier, C., (1836). *An Account of the War in Portugal between Don Pedro and D. Miguel.* Vols I & II (London: T. & W. Boone, 1836).

Lorette, J., *Les Expeditions militaires belges au Portugal en 1832 et 1833* (Brussels: Editions Universitaires, 1951).

Omboni, T., *Guerra Liberal 1832-1834, Avvenimenti militari e politici dell'ultimo mezzo seculo dell Portogallo* (Torino: Revista Enciclopedica Italiana, 1855).

O Arauto Portuense. 17th November-15th December (Porto: Typographia Gandra e Filhos, 1832).

The Annual Register, or a view of the History, Politics and Literature of the year 1833 (London: Baldwin & Cradock; J.G. & F. Rivingston, 1834).

Owen, H., *The Civil War in Portugal and the Siege of Porto* (London: Edward Moxon, 1836).

Saint-Pardoux, Baron de, *Campagnes de Portugal en 1833 et 1834. Relations des principaux évènements et des operations militaires de cette guerre* (Paris: Depot Central de La Librairie et de La Musique, 1835).

Shaw, C., *Personal Memoirs and Correspondence of Colonel Charles Shaw K.C.T.S. of the Portuguese Service* (London: Henry Colburn Publisher, 1847).

Soriano, S.J.L., *História da Guerra Civil.* Tomes I to VI (Lisboa: Imprensa Nacional, 1887).

Knight, T., *The British Battalion at Oporto with adventures, anecdotes, and exploits in Holland; at Waterloo and the expedition to Portugal* (London: Waugh & Innes; Edinburgh: Thomas Murray, Glasgow, 1834).

Unpublished Sources

Silva, J.M.M., 'A Marinha de Guerra Portuguesa desde o regresso de D. João VI a Portugal e o início da Regeneração (1821-1851) – Adaptação a uma nova realidade', Masters Thesis (Lisbon: University of Lisbon, 2009).